FAMILY TIES

OLD QUILT PATTERNS FROM
NEW CLOTH

Family Ties

Old Quilt Patterns from New Cloth

NANCILU BUTLER BURDICK

RUTLEDGE HILL PRESS

NASHVILLE, TENNESSEE

For Michelle

Published in Nashville, Tennessee, by Rutledge Hill Press, Inc., 513 Third Avenue South, Nashville, Tennessee 37210. Distributed in Canada by H. B. Fenn & Company, Ltd., Mississauga, Ontario.

Typography: Bailey Typography, Inc., Nashville, Tennessee
Book Design: Harriette Bateman
Photography by Nancilu B. Burdick unless otherwise noted.
Line drawings of patterns by Michelle Fitch.

Library of Congress Cataloging-in-Publication Data

Burdick, Nancilu B., 1917–
    Family ties : old quilt patterns from new cloth / Nancilu B. Burdick.
        p.   cm.
    Includes bibliographical references and index.
    ISBN 1-55853-134-3
    1. Quilting—Patterns.   2. Patchwork—Patterns.   3. Appliqué—Patterns.   4. Bottoms, Talula Gilbert, 1862–1946.   I. Title.
TT835.B83   1991
746.9′7′092—dc20   91-21340
                                                                      CIP

2 3 4 5 6 7 8 — 97 96 95 94 93 92
Printed in Hong Kong through Palace Press.

PREFACE

*F*amily journals and letters, a visit to a quilt exhibition, and a grandmother's quilts in her possession prompted Nancilu Burdick to begin to recreate the history of Talula Gilbert Bottoms and her quiltmaking. Little did she anticipate that the quest for Talula's quilts would eventually lead her from north to south and east to west, crisscrossing the country several times. In the process she found relatives previously unknown to her, and she found dozens of quilts made by the remarkable woman who was her grandmother.

She presented the early research in a paper, "Talula Gilbert Bottoms and Her Quilts," in 1984 at an American Quilt Study Group seminar in San Rafael, California, but that was only the beginning. Each discovery led to another, possibly with more discoveries still to come, and it was exhilarating to watch the extension of Talula's quilt connection across the continent.

Nancilu continued to sift through an immense collection of material, eliminating all but the most relevant, to tell the tale in *Legacy: The Story of Talula Gilbert Bottoms and Her Quilts*. The poignant details of Talula's early life, the hardships she endured with her beloved husband, and her devotion to her large family are entwined with a life of quiltmaking that sustained her in even the most difficult times. The hours she spent stitching brought peace to her heart, and in each completed task she found satisfaction and delight.

I met Nancilu when she wrote to me after viewing an exhibition called *Quilt Close-up: Five Southern Views* I had organized at the Folk Art Center in Asheville, North Carolina. Essays in the accompanying catalog described several families of quiltmakers, among them my own grandmother and her talents. The exhibit and catalog seemed to provide a focus for Nancilu to begin to organize a vast amount of family memorabilia into a meaningful record. As our correspondence continued, I had the pleasure of seeing her findings evolve into *Legacy*.

The discoveries did not end with the publication of the book. Along the way, its author had a desire to experience the craft from which Talula received such enjoyment. Reproducing and reinterpreting some of the patterns from her grandmother's collection, she added a new dimension to her own life. She was receiving, in a new age, the same benefits Talula had derived from her work.

Quilts are no longer thought of primarily as necessary bedcovering. Even so, their production has risen phenomenally since the late 1960s. Obviously our hands need to function, to express our creative minds, extending our being to the production of useful and lasting objects. From Talula's legacy Nancilu has experienced an enriching knowledge of herself, and she generously shares it with others so that they, too, may find the same rewards.

—Bets Ramsey

CONTENTS

PART I - PIECED QUILTS

PART II - PIECED AND APPLIQUÉ QUILTS

PART III - APPLIQUÉ QUILTS

ACKNOWLEDGMENTS

*H*ow far in time and space must we come, to old age perhaps if we are fortunate, to realize the magnitude of gifts received from generations of mothers and grandmothers who have left their legacy of creativity, courage, and endurance in their handmade quilts? To them I owe unspeakable gratitude, but it is to the living I wish to acknowledge my grateful appreciation here.

First, heartfelt thanks to five quiltmakers who contributed their ideas and skills in the quilts and quilt pieces made to illustrate this book: Michelle Fitch, who drafted the patterns and was the catalyst for this entire project; Frances Vining; Barbara Nagel; Fay Joerg; and Dorothy Frost. They also advised and encouraged me when my enthusiasm wavered. Special thanks to Frances, Michelle, and Hertha Ganey, Professor Emeritus of SUNY College at Buffalo, for reading an early version of the manuscript and making helpful suggestions.

Gratitude too deep for words is due my sister Ruth Butler Potts, who repeatedly loaned me treasured photographs, quilts, and her collection of Talula's quilt patterns and catalogs; my sisters Bettie Butler Pearson and Mary Alice Butler for photographs and sharing family scrapbooks and heirlooms; my sisters-in-law, Louise Martin Butler, Marguerite Reed Butler, and Grace Frink (Butler) Rabatin, their husbands and children, who shared quilts, memories, and lodging in my travels; Talula's foster son Carl Leake, who at age eighty was my guide in revisiting the Limestone County Bottoms homesteads and cemetery near Athens, Alabama; and his daughter Carol Hampton and her sisters who trusted me with a much-valued quilt; my Fayetteville, Georgia, Gilbert cousins George Hugh and Pauline Stell, Mildred and Charlie Fincher, and Nannie Lou Huie, descendants of Talula's beloved half-sister Bettie; John and Brenda Lynch, who shared their rare discovery in 1989 of John's great grandmother (Talula's sister) Nannie Gilbert Dickson's treasury of quilts and quilt tops and provided slides of some; my niece Donna Sue Barnhart; all my Bottoms cousins, especially Shirley and Peter Vandepoll, Margaret and Charles Avery, Roger, Jeanette, and Dafydd Bottoms, who loaned quilts or slides; and my Uncle Gilbert and Aunt Mayme, whose examples of generosity, love, fortitude, and unwavering faith in God have strengthened my own faith and resolve.

Always I have felt the encouragement and support of the whole body of the Emissary Foundation International, particularly the family at King View Farm; the Board of Directors and the members of the American Quilt Study Group, who have inspired me in their seminars and publications by their high standards of scholarship in quilt research; of that group particularly Barbara Brackman, whose *Encyclopedia of Pieced Quilt Patterns* has been an invaluable resource; and Bets Ramsey, who first introduced me to Rutledge Hill Press, encouraged me every step of the way, and honored my efforts by writing the preface to this book.

In addition, much credit is due the friends behind the scenes: Sara Walling and DeWitt Fowler, who transcribed on computer many pages and revisions of the handwritten text; DeWitt, Peter Vandepoll, and my dear friend Barbara Nagel, who assisted me in photography; Nancy Hoyler, Judy Farnham, and Martha Ferguson, owners of quilt shops who guided me in the selection of fabrics; the Millers, two skilled and dedicated quilters; and Barbara Bennett for the accurate transparencies of the quilt patterns.

My deepest gratitude goes to my children Sandra, James, and Christopher, and their families for love and encouragement and to my husband, Kenneth Rankin, without whose patience, devotion, companionship, skill in craftmanship, and thousands of miles of travel with me this project could never have been completed.

Finally, I have been most fortunate to have had the support and encouragement of a publisher with a vision and fine artistic standards. The energetic and talented staff of Rutledge Hill Press have been partners in producing this book and also friends.

INTRODUCTION

*T*his book presents thirty-eight quilt patterns based on the work of one woman, my grandmother, whose quiltmaking spanned eight decades in the Southeast, from the 1870s through 1945. Talula Gilbert was born near Atlanta, Georgia, during the Civil War, lost her mother before she was four, and as a child taught herself to quilt during the bitter years of the Reconstruction. Sensitive and intelligent, yet burdened with household duties and responsibilities for younger siblings, she had little formal education, all of it acquired in intermittent attendance at the one-room Gilbert Schoolhouse, a log structure her father had built on his farm in Fayette County. Nonetheless, she began early to write, as well as piece quilts, to assuage grief and unbearable heartache. In 1883 at age twenty-one she married Tom Bottoms, her childhood sweetheart and a struggling farmer subject to chronic attacks of malaria. By 1898 she had borne nine children, buried two infant sons, and lost other significant family members to death.

Talula was thirty-eight and had made numerous quilts when the family moved to the healthier climate of Sand Mountain in Cullman County, Alabama. But their "new home" was merely shelter, an old, cramped, and unpainted house on an isolated, unimproved and rocky hill farm. Making a living required grueling work and constant toil. There three more children were born, and another infant son died before Talula herself became desperately ill and had to spend four months in a sanitarium. Finally they moved sixty miles north to a larger, more fertile farm in Limestone County, where for a time they prospered. Throughout the years, Talula found solace in piecing quilts and in writing and receiving innumerable letters. When Talula died in 1946, she left as her legacy a memoir written in old age, hundreds of saved letters, and scores of quilts scattered from one end of the United States to the other.

As a material record of her place and time and a way of life almost forgotten, Talula's writings and her 130 extant quilts reflect her own ingenuity, courage, and perseverance and that of innumerable women, our forebears. These very quilts, predominantly handmade, inspired me to write her story, to become a quilter, and to make a vital connection with my ancestors and their living descendants. From years of travel to find and photograph Talula's quilts, the information I gathered from relatives verifies that she made more than two hundred in her lifetime.

Since the publication of *Legacy: The Story of Talula Gilbert Bottoms and Her Quilts,*[1] I am often asked two questions. The first usually is, "As a southern farm wife without modern conveniences, how was one woman able to make so many beautiful quilts and raise a large family?" The second is simply "Are her patterns available?" This book provides many of those patterns and suggests that, in fact, her quiltmaking did enable Talula Bottoms to raise her large family, to rise above grief and loss, and to live a long and fruitful life with grace and efficiency. In modest, often severe circumstances, from the desperate years after the Civil War through World War I and the Great Depression until the close of World War II, she found joy in making quilts and in giving them away.

At her death Talula left more than three hundred pages of quilt patterns, including catalogs and other sources of quilt designs. Before printed patterns were available, she had borrowed quilts she admired from others to draft the designs herself. The patterns in this book and the quilts made from them have been created from those sources: directly from Talula's existing quilts; from the paper patterns perforated with pin holes that she herself used, and from her own collection of patterns, leaflets, and flyers saved from needlecraft suppliers and newspaper columns.

Instead of giving her energies to bitterness and struggle against her hard circumstances, Talula turned increasingly to the creative outlet of quiltmaking. By losing herself in absorbing work, she became a creator and an artist. This book is a result of my learning from her that it is in the *doing* of things that transformation becomes possible. In the tangible act of crafting a product, people discover the truth of themselves, that as creators they are part of a rich and enduring tradition. Moreover, the present quilt movement can be understood as a natural cycle of history, softening the hard edges of technology and the impersonality of machine-made things.[2] As creators, our hands learning as we improve our skills, we know we are links in a chain of craftsmanship that should not be broken.

To recreate and interpret Talula's patterns in contemporary fabrics, I enlisted the help of several friends who are

Several pattern booklets collected by Talula

experienced quiltmakers. The quilts and patterns shown on the following pages reflect many hours of cooperative work during which we were inspired by each other's various and creative approaches in using the old-time patterns. We have discovered how our hands are willing to learn from a challenging pattern. Moreover, we have found that quiet work done at the end of a busy day, while traveling or waiting, or as a day-long productive activity, engenders stillness of mind and heart and nourishes creative energy, resulting in more emotional and physical strength to transcend obstacles and face the challenges life brings. We remember that we have inherited the strength and endurance of a people whose courage and skills we can nurture in ourselves, extend to those around us, and pass on to future generations. Working in contemporary fabrics with traditional designs that have withstood the test of time, we have found them equally adaptable to producing explosions of color and imagination or to replicating quilts made by our grandmothers. The patterns and quilt illustrations are offered in the hope that other quiltmakers, whatever their procedures and levels of skill, will find them a stimulus for like inspiration.

The quilt patterns illustrated range from easier to more challenging. The "Pieced Quilts" section, for instance, begins with the *Snowball*, a pattern often used by our grandmothers to introduce very young girls to curved-patch piecing. The "Pieced and Appliqué" section moves from easier to more complex constructions. The "Appliqué" section, however, is offered randomly, because any quilter can see at a glance a pattern's appeal and skill level.

Each pattern is illustrated with one or more examples recently handmade in today's fabrics and colors. All have been tested for accuracy and pleasure in piecing or appliquéing by hand. Of course, many of the patterns can also be adapted to quick-cutting and machine piecing. The book represents the work and talents of several skilled quilters adept in use of the sewing machine, who nevertheless subscribe to the value, the sense of purpose, and the pleasure to be found in hand-piecing, appliqué, and quilting.

In addition to the new examples of the old quilt patterns, a number of Talula's family quilts are illustrated. Stories of the quilts—who they were made for if known, where they "lived" and traveled, and reference to the patterns' origins—encompass history and traditions from the Civil War through World War II. They reflect resourcefulness and illustrate a love of quiltmaking many quilters can identify with today. For Talula Bottoms, whose hands were never idle, quiltmaking enriched and prolonged her life, and the quilts she left have strengthened family ties among her scores of descendants.

Handmade quilts can still cross generations to provide for individuals and families those same benefits even in our own fast-moving and uncertain world.

FAMILY TIES

OLD QUILT PATTERNS FROM NEW CLOTH

CONTINUING THE TRADITION

The American genius for creating machines has often
deprived us of many activities which are the source of
much pleasure and satisfaction, for machines have been
permitted to take over some of the creative crafts in
addition to those involving drudgery.[1]

*I*n the first half of the twentieth century, at least up to
World War II when mothers were working outside the
home in large numbers, it was customary for girls to learn to
sew by hand before being allowed to use the sewing machine. Unlike then, quilt teachers today often find that stu-
dents born after World War II come to class able to sew
quite respectably on the sewing machine but have never
been taught to hold a needle, wear a thimble, or sew a
straight seam by hand.[2] The whole tradition of hand sewing
is in danger of being lost to them. It seems important, therefore, to evaluate the present attitude of promoting greater
speed in quiltmaking through more sophisticated technology. To appreciate our heritage, we need to consider the
value of the total creative process.

The notion that "every generation has its tasks, and it is
the task of our generation to find our roots"[3] has become
increasingly prevalent since the publication in 1976 of Alex
Haley's landmark book *Roots*.[4] The significance of this idea
cannot be overestimated. The need to connect with our
human roots is even greater today as technology "has sepa-
rated us from our environment and from each other in ways
that can only be called unnatural."[5] Though most of us may
not be able to trace our personal roots to their source as
Haley did, we can connect with our human roots in a variety
of ways. More and more people are engaging in traditional
crafts as a way of linking to the past.

As individuals we are a part of a larger whole, past and
present, of the human family. We live and move and create
along a continuum that began in the distant past and will go
on long after we are no longer here. We have a responsibility
to pass on to those who come after us something of the skills
and traditions of those who came before, affirming history
as a living thing of which we are a part rather than a "force"
over which we have no control.[6] We are making quilts not
merely to decorate our surroundings or win honors, but to
contribute to something greater than ourselves. In whatever
we do we are accountable for what we leave as a record of

our having lived—in short, for our own small segment of
human history.[7]

We quilters can choose to use our hands and talents to
create beauty as our ancestors did, and we can keep those
vital skills alive for our own and future generations. In
quiltmaking, although we do not always work as the early
quilters did, we remember and demonstrate to our children
our infinite debt to those who first developed quilting skills,
designs, and techniques. How amazed our grandparents
would be to know that today a worldwide, diverse, and significant interest in quilts has evolved! And yet we can become carried away by the very size of the quilt industry and
its popularity, forgetting its more profound function as a
bridge across generations.

In a culture increasingly automated, increasingly clut-
tered with "disposables" mass-produced in synthetic materials and untouched by human hands, we need to know we
can still make a vital connection with our human forebears.
In handcrafts we discover an endless source of beauty and
learning, an outlet for continuing creativity, and a sense of
purpose that goes beyond ownership and lifestyle. We can
actually experience ourselves as creators, not merely collectors and consumers.

Our grandparents' generation knew that anything of
value takes time, that in any creative work the process itself
is invested with pleasure and offers healing perspective on
the concerns and problems that inevitably arise in the business of living. For them, craftsmanship was essential to
comfort, health, and survival, and in using natural materials
they were connected to their source of life in the earth. At
the same time, working long hours with skilled hands enabled them to transcend their physical circumstances. They
knew, perhaps unconsciously, that the *touching* and the *time*
spent in making a thing invests it with the substance of their
own spirit, a substance that lives on and speaks for them
long after their voices and their hands are silent and still.

In China's Yellow River basin a museum was built over

the site of the six-thousand-year-old matriarchal Ban Po Village, where fragments of utensils and artifacts are left untouched by excavation tools, the site only partially excavated to reveal the handiwork of those ancient people. Theirs was not a throwaway culture, for the work of their hands was saved, often buried with the maker. Clay pots, bone needles, and fragments of woven baskets and cloth are reminders that the long history of creating with the hands began with our earliest human ancestors. Their artifacts were valued as if they were sacred extensions of the people who made them.

Remembering who we are and where we came from can add purpose and meaning to our daily pursuits of work and recreation. A resulting sense of humility and wholeness may even contribute to health and sanity.

The therapeutic value of quiltmaking was recognized by physicians and others more than half a century ago. "No artificial exercise can equal that . . . of creating beauty with your own hands," said Ruth E. Finley in 1931. "Quiltmaking has . . . deep roots of interest which strike back into the history of America as does no other craft." It is, she said, "an ideal prescription for nerves, or general lack of interest in life."[8]

Dr. William Rush Dunton, Jr., physician to "nervous ladies" and quilt historian, who attributed his earliest interest in quilts to assisting his mother in cutting small diamonds from his own silk neckties in the late 1870s, made the point more specifically in 1946. It is "the stimulus of color" and the concentration required to form accurate patterns, as well as "in making a quilt block [one] has no time to worry over fancied ill health . . . or wrongs and slights which may be real. . . ."[9]

Today all ages, as well as social and economic groups of women and some men who never considered themselves creative, are discovering they are creative through quiltmaking. Their increased self-esteem then affects in a positive way not only their families, but all those with whom they come in contact. Craftsmanship, suggests M. C. Richards, "may foster a healing of those inner divisions which set [people] at war with [themselves] and therefore with others."[10]

More recently, Kristen Langellier has made the point that women's absorption in quiltmaking, conceiving the idea for a quilt and bringing it into form as a finished product, can be associated with images of birth: "Giving birth to the quilt and giving birth to the true self." Such self-realization transforms by making very tangible her creative capacities.[11] Consequently, the ability to overcome feelings of grief and loss when tragedies strike is greatly enhanced. All these benefits for women then accrue to families, bringing them closer in values and appreciation of each other.

It seems we lose more than we know if we do not experience at times the creative process of working with nothing between the hands and materials except the essential tools. Such activity intimately connects us with the past, and by

Ruth Butler (age 4) learning to sew

example we demonstrate our respect for tradition and build closer family ties across generations. As Patsy and Myron Orlofsky say, quilting by hand has "continued uninterrupted almost as it originally evolved—it has never depended upon a professional class for its skills."[12] Today handwork in quilting is still highly valued. Numerous ordinary people and trained artists who are also professional quilters continue the tradition of working by hand, even though there is "a professional class" of machine quilters as well.

Other advantages of handwork have often been noted; today many quilters keep their portable needlework in a state of readiness for travel and sundry occasions when hands would otherwise lie idle and the time seem tedious or wasted. Some would still agree with one of America's greatest presidents. Thomas Jefferson, in a 1787 letter, reminded his daughter Martha, while she was in school in France, of the "democratic virtues" in needlework:

In the country life of America there are many moments when a woman can have recourse to nothing but her needle for employment. In a dull company, and in dull weather, for instance, it is ill-manners to read, it is ill-manners to leave them; no card-playing there among genteel people. . . . the needle is then a valuable resourse [sic].[13]

Of course quiltmaking by machine has its place and plays an increasingly important role in people's lives today—especially for women who must juggle career, homemaking, and child care with their needs for creative expression—and for many who are professional quiltmakers. In addition, some of the most original, impressively beautiful, and ingenious textile art pieces, quilts that are winning prizes all over the world, have been entirely machine pieced, appliquéd, and quilted. "One also wonders," suggests Dianne Miller, "if art quilts (such as those) made by a Ruth McDowell or a Michael James can actually be made by hand."[14]

But with speed so emphasized today, do we need to be reminded that even from its beginnings the sewing machine was a mixed blessing for women? Industrialists quickly exploited it for profit, and cottage industries were replaced by sweatshops where women themselves became cogs in the wheels of industry.[15] How different then were the lives of women formerly occupied in their own homes creating for their families both clothing and quilts in a quiet, peaceful atmosphere. The machine had relieved them of much drudgery in utility sewing, men's suits and work clothes as well as the many everyday quilts and children's clothing needed for large families. But after the middle to late nineteenth century, when machine-stitching was even proudly displayed on "best quilts," the novelty had worn off. The sewing machine had ceased to be a status symbol; it was taken for granted as "simply that—a machine," and handwork again became valued for its own sake.[16] Even today many quilters who normally sew by machine will choose to make a quilt by hand if it is to be a wedding present or saved as an heirloom. They feel that handwork confers a timeless value on the product.

The patterns here are offered both for those who choose to sew by hand in an atmosphere of quiet reflection and for those who, as one quilter expressed it, find a different kind of pleasure and excitement in working with the sewing machine. "Seeing the *Flying Geese* flying out from under the needle of my machine was like watching the migration north of those majestic birds in the spring. The speed was part of the thrill, and it felt like a very natural thing I was doing."[17] In either case, we can realize that what we are creating, and the process itself, connects us with our original ancestors as far back in time as human history extends; the knowledge that we are continuing the tradition lends significance to our work.

Detail of Goose Tracks   *(1985)*   *Nancilu Burdick*

Fayette County Courthouse, c. 1909 photograph. Built in 1827, it is the oldest county courthouse in Georgia, having narrowly escaped burning by the "hated Yankees" in 1864. The clock tower was added in 1880, but the clock itself was not installed until 1909. The photograph was sent to Tom and Talula Bottoms in Alabama by their niece Mollie. They kept it as a treasured reminder of where Tom bought the marriage license in February 1883 before he and Talula were "tied up in the marriage vow" (Legacy, 65).

In any age we live both our individual lives and the life of our times. We cannot turn back the clock or ignore the remarkable technology that offers us such wide choices of process and reduces the time for making a quilt. Nor can we forget that economic necessity may affect our choices. Many quilters are "working women" who use this technology to run a profitable business while they savor the creative expression of doing what they most enjoy. Yet even they occasionally yearn to practice the ancient skills of handwork, continuing the tradition that lends perspective in a fast-moving world. Moreover, with so much emphasis on speed and technology, especially for those who are not professionals, it is helpful to know that handwork is still a choice, and in an atmosphere of quiet and meditation one's sense of the value of life is enhanced. Remembering who we are, we realize that the process is invested with as much meaning as the product; and we come closer to nature (and to each other), as someone has said, in form, in spirit, and in truth—in other words, closer to ourselves and to our roots. Neither the hum of a motor nor the clatter of machinery comes between us and the quiet process of creation. And even though the fabric, the needles, the thread, and the objects we use to cut and mark the patches are factory made, we ourselves need not feel pressured to become like machines, turning out our products with ever-increasing speed just to finish them quickly. Instead, we can quietly reflect with awe and appreciation on the natural potential in our hands, so marvelously made as they always have been for the most intricate and creative work. Regardless of the craft or art form, when we make such a connection with our true selves, there is something one person might call magic, another spiritual transformation, that enters the process, and we find the fragments of our lives fitting into meaningful patterns.

PART I

Detail of Indian Wedding Ring   (c. 1891)   *Talula Gilbert Bottoms*

PIECED QUILTS

While many quilters find hand-piecing most pleasurable and relaxing, others need the stimulus of making their blocks more quickly by machine. Whether one uses one method or the other, or a combination of both, choosing fabrics and planning a quilt must be followed by routine work: washing and ironing, cutting the pieces, and, when necessary, marking the seams. The latter can be the tedious phase of quiltmaking, and some choose to mark only enough pieces at one time for a few blocks. Then on to the real joy of piecing, watching the blocks one by one take shape, the pieces coming together into orderly patterns, urged on by hands that were made to create the beauty our souls need to thrive. A well-known contemporary psychologist said, "Beauty is essential to the health of the soul,"[1] and each quilt conceived and brought to form is an individual expression of that innate need, regardless of the method used to create it. The word *work* then takes on a more vital and joyful meaning, for we are all potential artists. We do not need to "thank God it's Friday," for by losing ourselves in the creative act, we have transcended time and circumstances; all our hours and days are filled with excitement and purpose.

For those who need specific directions for piecing a quilt, books with procedures and instructions abound. Here directions are kept to a minimum, leaving decisions regarding process to each person. Some sources I have found useful are indicated in the Bibliography. One should remember, however, that *seam allowances need to be added* to each pattern piece. I like to cut from template plastic two patterns for each piece, one with seams added, and one just the size for marking the sewing lines.

Detail of unquilted Maple Leaf *(1991) Nancilu Burdick*

SNOWBALL (1990) Michelle Fitch

TALULA SAVED two *Snowball* quilts handmade by her daughters, who took entirely different paths in life: Mollie Ruth—writer, lecturer, and revered professor of English at Oklahoma State University at Edmond; and Almira—fine needlewoman, community leader, dutiful farm wife, and mother of eight children. Mollie Ruth recorded in her journal, "[We] grew up on a farm in Alabama, in a family with no literary pretensions—knew birds and flowers and trees by name—could pick blackberries, hull walnuts, and make patchwork quilts, but knew nothing about Ulysses, Siegfried or even Little Nell."[2] As soon as Talula's daughters were able to buy blankets, they looked back at their own quiltmaking and their quilts as representing a way of life they were glad to leave behind.

Talula had used the different *Snowball* patterns to introduce her young daughters to curved-patch piecing, after they had pieced at least one simpler top that was "worth quilting" (a four- or nine-patch without curves). One was pieced in Cullman County, Alabama, by Mollie Ruth "when I was about seven or eight years old . . . it was not even the first quilt I made that was considered worth quilting. . . . It is not worth keeping and protecting."[3] The workmanship is a child's and the uneven quilting in shells suggests it was quilted at a quilting party such as Mollie Ruth described in 1939 in one of the journals she kept throughout her life: "In the midst of the summer at layin' by time, quiltings and log-rollings were companion activities. Then the routine work of farm families would take on a festive character."[4] The noon meal, served outdoors on long tables under the trees, was the primary event of the day. There was no partying in the evening—or dancing either—for those pious people of the "Bible Belt" South.

Mollie Ruth's quilt is a curved four-patch,[5] Almira's a center curved nine-patch set into corner pieces to make a square (*Legacy*, 101). Almira's pattern is given here.

Mollie Ruth and Almira (1910)

When Talula realized her daughters so heartily disliked quiltmaking they were willing to do anything to avoid it, she folded their quilts safely away. Almira's *Snowball* was never washed and probably little used; Mollie Ruth decided, after her mother's death, to take hers to Oklahoma for everyday cover. Both would be inherited later by two of Almira's daughters. Thus the *Snowball* quilts provided an unbroken bridge across generations of women in Talula's family.

Snowball *(1990)*
Michelle Fitch

4

The block is easy to assemble in three steps. First, make the circle in three strips (an unequal nine-patch). Second, sew the four corner pieces together in two units by joining each at a center seam. Third, pin-baste the corner units, one at a time, and stitch to the circle, before joining the last two open seams. For a full-size quilt, make thirty blocks and assemble with three-inch sashing. Block size: 11 inches.

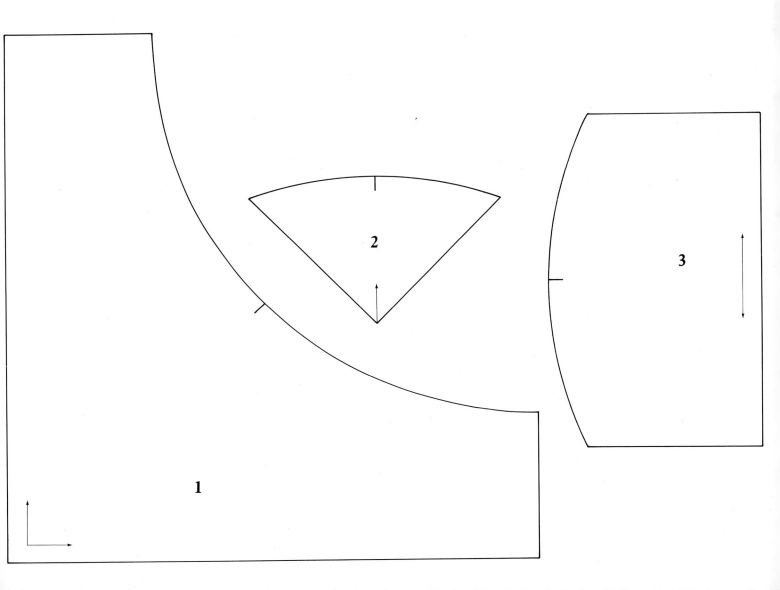

2

3

1

MAPLE LEAF (c. 1910)   Talula Gilbert Bottoms

IT HAS OFTEN been said that the essence and spirit of the quiltmaker can be felt in the work of her hands. Quilts much used and little noticed during a maker's lifetime are often washed and carefully folded away at her death to be saved for future generations. It seems to be both a part of the ritual of mourning and a manner of preserving the spirit and essence of the loved one—to thus assuage grief and loss.

The *Maple Leaf,* made from a Clara Stone pattern published in *Practical Needlework* in 1910, was filled with thick, hand-carded cotton and quilted in shells. It was among a dozen or more quilts Talula gave to her daughter Almira for everyday use with her large family. After many years of service, the humble quilt was put away at Talula's death. In the big Butler farm house, unheated except for fireplaces and the kitchen woodstove, there were five bedrooms and a sleeping porch and ten people who needed warm covers on cold winter nights. Talula's quilts, which she continued to make by hand until shortly before her death in 1946, provided most of that cover. Almira's daughter-in-law, Grace Butler Rabatin, recalls:

> I remember how wonderful it was to go home, when Bob was in the Army (1945), and sleep under a pile of those colorful old quilts Grandma had made. Then one time after the war we went home and the quilts had just vanished. They had been replaced by new wool blankets. I wondered at the time what had happened to them. It was years later I realized they had all been put away to save as soon as Grandma passed away. I never saw those quilts again until Mother Butler died in 1980.[6]

Grace's daughter inherited the *Maple Leaf* with its visible sewing machine stitching on the stems. Well-worn and often washed, it is yet treasured to become an heirloom for Talula's great-great granddaughter.

Maple Leaf *unquilted top*   *(1991)*   *Nancilu Burdick*

Maple Leaf   *(1910)*   *Talula Gilbert Bottoms*

For a full-size quilt piece thirty nine-patch blocks. To assemble with "streaks of lightning" sashing, cut fifty-four triangular half squares longsides on straight of grain, and twelve quarter squares, allowing one-fourth-inch extra width on the long sides in addition to the seam allowance. Assemble in vertical strips, alternating the patterned half-blocks at top and bottom. Block size: 10 inches.

Stem

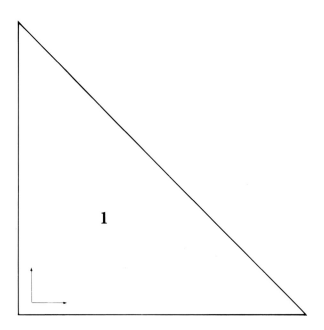

1

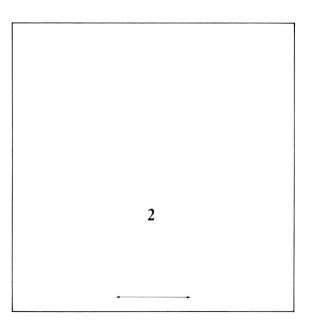

2

ROCKY ROAD TO KANSAS (1990) Michelle Fitch

TALULA'S WEDDING gift in 1940 to this author, her fifth granddaughter and the first one to have a "real wedding" to which her grandparents were invited, was a silk and wool *Crazy* quilt, the only one of those Victorian beauties Talula is known to have made. In addition to the wood-filled, lavishly embroidered quilt, Talula gave five quilt tops to her daughter Almira to quilt or have quilted for the author's hope chest. The *Rocky Road to Kansas* string quilt is one of those.

Almira, with sincere desire to manifest her love by adding her own handwork to that of her mother, bravely dusted off and set up her old quilting frame and put in Talula's version of the *Rocky Road to Kansas*, feeling the work would go rapidly though she had long before lost both interest and skill in quilting. She made false starts, working awkwardly in whatever direction her fingers would go until her wrists were sore and fingers pricked and bleeding. After the third day, with the quilting hardly begun and feeling the work was "driving her almost crazy," she called in Miss Mary Sutton whom she had paid to quilt mattress pads for $1.50 each. Miss Mary was in her seventies and lived in a log cabin on the Butler farm with a nephew and his wife, Bertha, who washed and ironed for Almira's large family for one dollar a week. Bertha and Miss Mary helped Almira take the unfinished quilt out of the frame to set it up in their own frame in the log cabin "up in the hollow" at the foot of Keel Mountain. Miss Mary charged $2.50 for quilting the *Rocky Road to Kansas;* then she quilted one more for Almira, a *Fancy Dresden Plate*, for which she charged three dollars. After that she "took to her bed with the fever, and a few weeks later she died."[7]

Rocky Road to Kansas, "colonial in inspiration but modern in usage," was called by Carrie A. Hall "the twentieth-century development of the crazy quilt in cotton pieces."[8] It has many possibilities in today's fabrics, as demonstrated, for instance, by Beth

Rocky Road to Kansas *(1990)   Nancilu Burdick*

Gutcheon's *Cynthia Ann Dancing*.[9] When made as a string quilt it closely resembles the *Rocky Road to Kansas* (Ladies Art Company #236 pattern) that Talula made earlier and gave to her half sister Bettie Stell when her twins were born in 1906.

Rocky Road to Kansas *(1990)   Michelle Fitch*

Bettie Stell's twins with Talula's quilt in background

The block is easily pieced by remembering to create pieces with seams as straight as possible. Make two corner units, then complete each half of the block as shown. Finally, join the two halves. Interesting patterns will emerge if the blocks are placed adjacent to each other and joined without sashing. Block size: 10 inches.

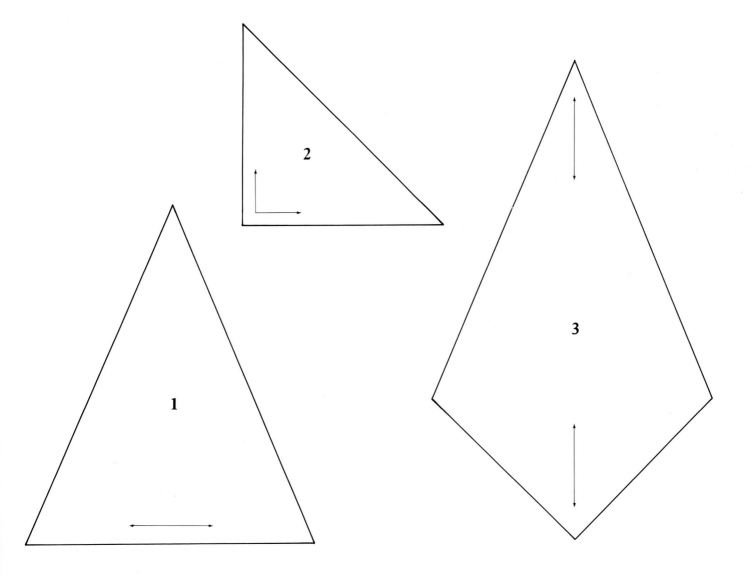

DIAMOND STAR *(Priscilla)* (1990) Michelle Fitch

TALULA'S HABIT, even after 1895 when her first treadle machine was bought, was to continue to piece or appliqué her quilt blocks by hand, assembling some by machine and others by hand. After almost thirty years of hard use, because nearly all clothing for the large family had been made at home, including the men's suits and work clothes, the old machine was replaced in the 1920s with a new Mason Rotary.

Talula must have tried piecing an entire quilt on her new machine, for in the *Diamond Star* made for her daughter Almira the only handwork aside from the quilting is the careful blind-stitching of the red binding. The large pattern and bold red, white, and blue colors in the everyday quilt made it appropriate for use on boys' beds.

Almira had hoped for a "small" family of four children, and when her fifth child and third boy arrived in 1922, she wondered where she would put them all. The farm home was soon enlarged—the roof raised to accommodate a large sleeping porch with windows all around two sides. The star quilt, as well as many other everyday quilts Talula made for her daughter's growing family, saw hard use on the sunny sleeping porch and many washings before it was put away to save for another generation, Talula's grandchildren.

Talula made at least one other *Diamond Star* in the 1930s. Her existing pattern, scored for tracing, appeared in *Eight Star Designs* that she ordered from *The Progressive Farmer and Southern Ruralist* some time between 1930 and 1935.[10] That version, with patches somewhat smaller than the ones in her 1920s quilt, is the one offered here.

Diamond Star *(c. 1920)* *Talula Gilbert Bottoms*

New Mason Rotary sewing machine (c. 1925). Talula used the machine until 1940 to sew her own clothes and "Papa's" nightshirts and underwear and to assemble scores of quilts after she had hand-pieced the blocks. (Photograph courtesy of Mary Wentworth)

Diamond Star *(Fitch)*

Assemble the pieces of this block into four units, then join to form the sixteen-inch block. The kaleidoscope effect is created by assembling the blocks without sashing. Block size: 16 inches.

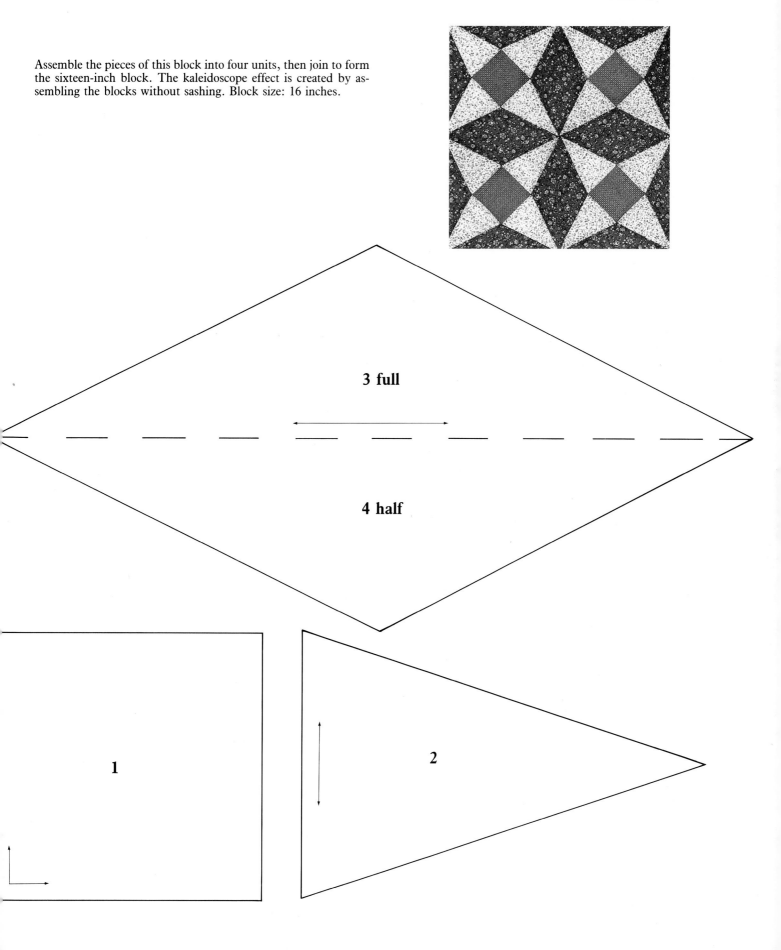

3 full

4 half

1

2

VARIABLE STAR *(Sapphire Star)* (1986) Nancilu Burdick★

STAR DESIGNS have always been perhaps the most perennial of all shapes used in quilts, with the eight-pointed star the most frequently seen. Forty-three of Talula's existing quilts are made in some version of the star pattern. Since it is an easily pieced pattern, she may have made a number of others for her children's families, quilts that saw hard use for family cover and were worn out. One of her granddaughters remembers that Talula almost always had a star quilt in process.

This simplest of *Variable Stars*, a design found in Talula's copy of *Quilt Patterns: Patchwork and Appliqué* (1928, Ladies Art Company), is ideal for a beginning quilter. The two quilts illustrated were both learning and healing projects, pieced by hand with unmarked seams. The *Sapphire Star,* made in memory of a son who died young, reflects the richness and intensity of his short life. It was begun in September 1985, on the anniversary of his birth, and the star blocks were completed six weeks later. The setting design was suggested by an old Georgian quilt (1820–1830) called *Evening Star.* A few leftover (light blue) stars became the starting point for the monochrome *Tranquility.*[11] Piecing the latter provided relaxing interludes between publisher's deadlines and the pressure of writing the final draft of *Legacy.*

Sapphire Star *(Burdick)*

Photograph of Talula and Tom Bottoms with great-grandson Victor Burdick, Jr. (April, 1943)

★The asterisk after the author's name in every case indicates that the quilt was quilted by Elizabeth and Kate Miller, professional quilters of rare skill and dedication.

Tranquility *(1987)* *Nancilu Burdick★*

This unequal nine-patch block is easily assembled in three units by sewing only straight seams. For a double coverlet-size quilt or one that will go to the dust ruffle of a three-quarter bed, make forty-two star blocks and assemble diagonally with thirty seven-inch plain squares, twenty-two half-squares, and four quarter-squares. For the saw-tooth border, use the three-inch triangle pattern to make 108 squares, alternating light and dark calicos. Block size: 7 inches.

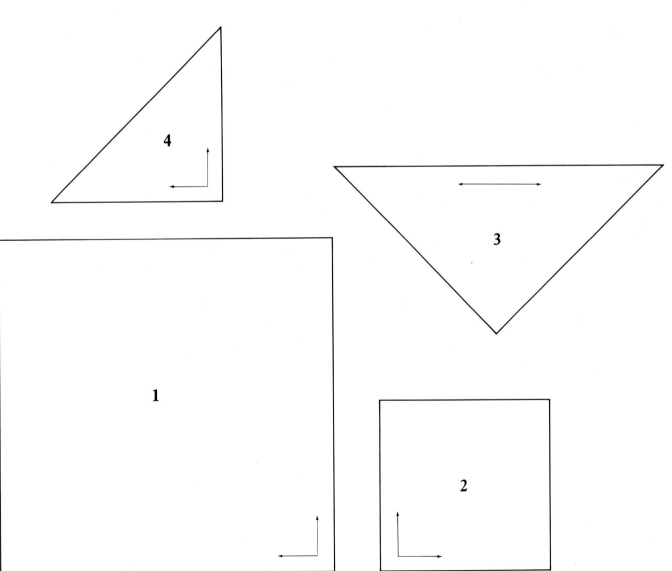

VICE PRESIDENT'S QUILT (1989) Fay Joerg

THE MODEL for Fay's quilts was the old quilt made in Fayette County, Georgia (c. 1875) by Talula's mother-in-law (*Legacy*, 76). Pieced from sewing scraps and from salvaged parts of worn-out clothes, it was set together with dyed feed-sack sashing, a hard-times quilt, indeed. Eliza McElroy Hartsfield was descended from two prominent Georgia families, the McElroys and the Hartsfields. In 1840 at age nineteen she married James Bottoms, an ambitious cotton planter who was also a descendant of the Hartsfields and a widower with eight children. Eliza had been taught fine needlework skills and was a superb weaver. While bearing eight more children to James Bottoms in the prosperous years before the Civil War, Eliza wove elegant coverlets and made many beautiful quilts. The war changed all that (*Legacy*, 57, 66). James Bottoms lost almost everything and sold two beloved slaves in order to leave "$200 in gold" to each of his children by his first wife and to pay debts left by the early death of his oldest son, John, to help the young widow and her five children survive in the Reconstruction. James died in 1866 from illness and grief brought on by the war. During the next eighteen years Eliza managed, through the most incredible ingenuity and resourcefulness, to hold on to her farm and make stunning scrap quilts from salvaged materials.

When it came to dividing Eliza's quilts in 1884, her youngest son, Tom, Talula's husband, "got only the poorest bunch." The *Vice President's Quilt* was one of those. But Talula and Tom treasured it so highly that they saved the much-used and faded utility quilt as an heirloom. The strong fabrics, some of them hand-woven, may outlast the new fabrics in quilts made today.

Whether or not this design received its name because of a particular vice president (Garret A. Hobard served with President McKinley in 1898 when the pattern was first published by the Ladies Art Company), it was an old pattern already. Simple to piece, the design lends itself to creative interpretations in today's fabrics. It can be assembled conventionally with sashing, or the blocks can be joined to form new patterns and images, as Fay's examples demonstrate.

Vice President's Quilt   *(Joerg)*

Vice President II   *(Joerg)*

To assemble the block, first make two corner units, and join them to the extra #4 pieces to make the smaller square. Then add the outside corner pieces to complete the nine-inch square. Block size: 9 inches.

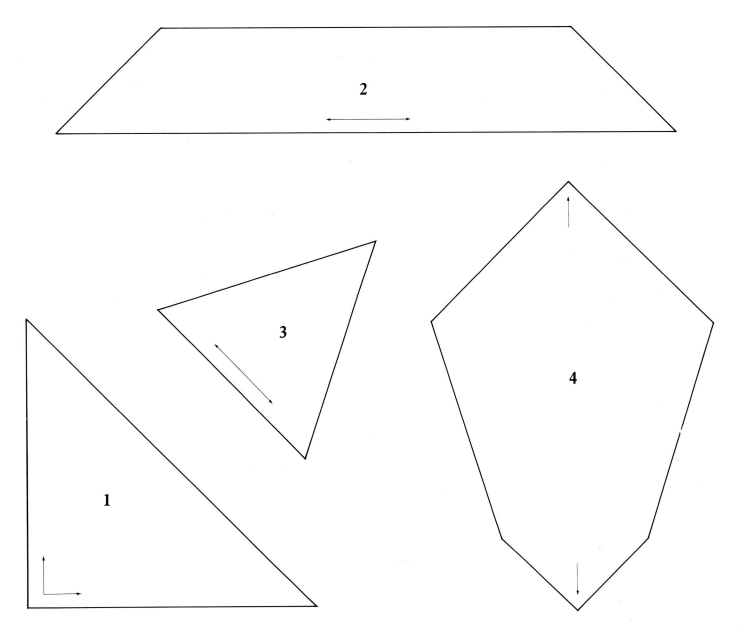

BETTIE'S SCRAP QUILT (1990) Group quilt, quilted by Barbara Phillippi

AN EARLY DESIGN called *Mosaic*, identical to this pattern, was published by the Ladies Art Company in 1898. Talula's old quilt, made in the first quarter of the twentieth century, lives up to that name, although more than likely she found the pattern in a farm publication or got it from friends or relatives (*Legacy*, 162). The quilt was rebound and put away after Talula's death, later to be inherited by her youngest granddaughter, Bettie Pearson, hence the name given it here. Much used and often washed, the old fabric remains bright, and the overall shifting pattern startles with its resemblance to contemporary art.

That quilt is one of a number of Talula's quilts filled with hand-carded cotton her husband raised on their own farm. She told her grandchildren that each child's task on winter days after school was to separate enough seeds from lint cotton to fill his or her shoe (the younger the child, the smaller the shoe). Their father used the seeds from the best bolls to develop his long-fibered "Bottoms Cotton Seed," sold widely to farmers and experiment stations in the Southeast during the 1920s (*Legacy*, 128). One year Tom Bottoms planted a crop of cotton in the front yard, up to the very edge of the imposing veranda of their new home, much to his daughters' embarrassment. So eager was he to prosper by using every inch of the fertile land on his Limestone County farm, after fifteen years of struggle on the rocky hill farm in Cullman County, he cared not a whit for the increasingly popular new status symbol of a well-trimmed green lawn.

When pieced in three strips across, the block pattern presented here is suitable for either easy and relaxed hand piecing or machine work. This new quilt was hand-pieced by the six women who produced patterns and examples for this book and signed as a friendship quilt to commemorate the joint effort. It was machine-assembled by the author and quilted by Barbara Phillippi.

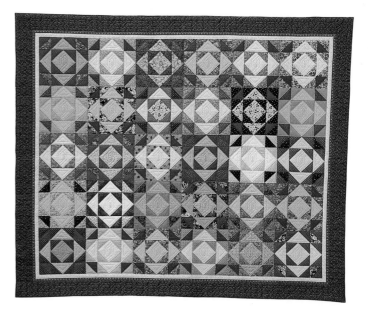

Bettie's Scrap Quilt

Cotton planted on "front lawn" of New Limestone County Bottoms home with the barrel for collecting "finest bolls" for Tom's horticultural experiments

Detail of Bettie's Scrap Quilt

I followed Talula's example by making this block in three strips across. If the completed blocks are joined horizontally without sashing, alternating the dark and lighter ones, the diagonal pattern emerges. A very narrow, light inner border emphasizes the diagonal effect. Block size: 12 inches.

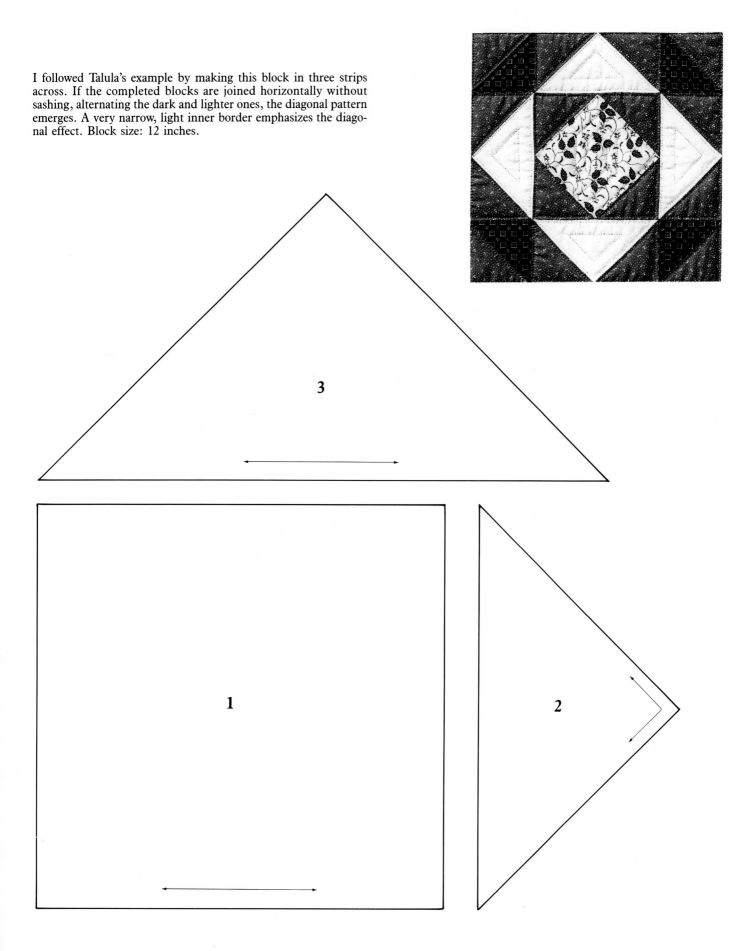

EASTERN STAR   (1989)   Pieced by Nancilu Burdick★

THIS NINETEENTH-CENTURY design, one that lent itself to creating impressive quilts from a scrap bag of innumerable and otherwise useless small pieces of leftover cloth, was often exchanged by country women in Georgia. Some of the stars in Talula's late 1800s quilt, from which the one illustrated here was designed, use eight different fabrics, and yet the quilt maintains a consistent pattern of light and dark that is, perhaps deliberately, broken only once (*Legacy*, 118). Such consistency of design illustrates both the creative use of castoffs by women of modest means and the essential need for beauty in drab surroundings.

Talula's sister-in-law, Susan Collins Bottoms, made an earlier *Eastern Star* that may have been the source of Talula's pattern. The older quilt found in Alabama with Susan's great-grandson is one of four surviving quilts made by Susan or by her daughter Mollie, who wrote hundreds of letters that were saved by Talula. Similar patterns from the Nancy Cabot Column in the *Chicago Tribune* were published by the *Progressive Farmer* in the 1930s and by C. W.

Calkins and Company for Clara Stone, who had earlier submitted numerous patterns to *Hearth and Home* magazine.

Generally the country women faced bare plank walls and floors. The latter were adorned, if at all, with their own homemade rugs; the kitchen floors were strewn with sand to absorb grease and tracked-in dirt, and the furniture was often homemade. In such an atmosphere of plainness, Talula's quilt was an everyday bedcovering that lifted the spirits of all who lived with it. Making such a quilt from leftover scraps of fabric can be equally satisfying today, whether it is pieced by hand or machine. Borderless, its old-fashioned charm gives life and character to an otherwise ordinary room.

The quilt illustrated here was entirely hand-pieced from cotton fabrics, precisely cut into triangles and squares with one-eighth-inch unmarked seams, and assembled by hand. The batting is wool, chosen to satisfy an urge to make one quilt wholly with natural materials.

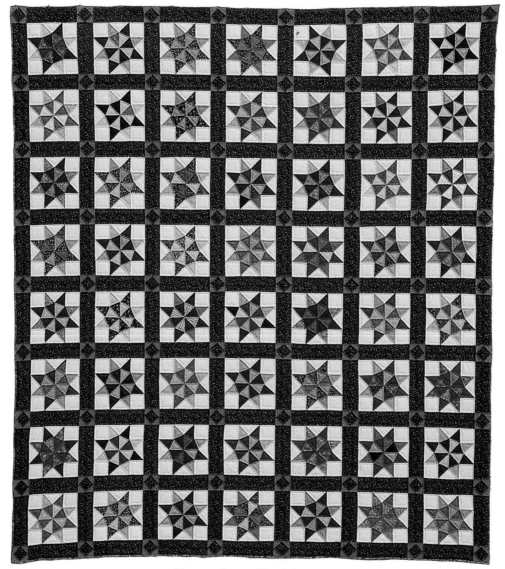

Eastern Star   (*Burdick*)

George Washington and Susan Collins Bottoms (seated) with their sons Claude (left) and Jim, their daughter Mollie (left) and visiting niece Almira Bottoms, Talula's daughter. The group posed beside the Fayette County log cabin George W. built in 1870 and still standing today. The unpainted clapboard was added in the 1880s to the front portion for insulation, preservation, and improvement of appearance. The young women's essential need for beauty is expressed in the lace curtains at the window, their silk dresses fashioned by their own hands, and doubtless Susan's and Mollie's colorful quilts on beds inside the plain rooms. It was Susan who made a Feather *quilt (c. 1850) from which Talula drafted the pattern for her own 1885* Feather.
Photograph c. 1910.

This is a variation of the *LeMoyne Star.* Join the #3 triangles to form diamonds. Sew these pieced diamonds into four units with the triangles. Then make two units by adding the squares and join them to complete the block. Assemble with sashing or adjacently as desired. Fifty-six blocks set together with two-and-one-half-inch sashing will make a double bed quilt. Block size: 8 inches.

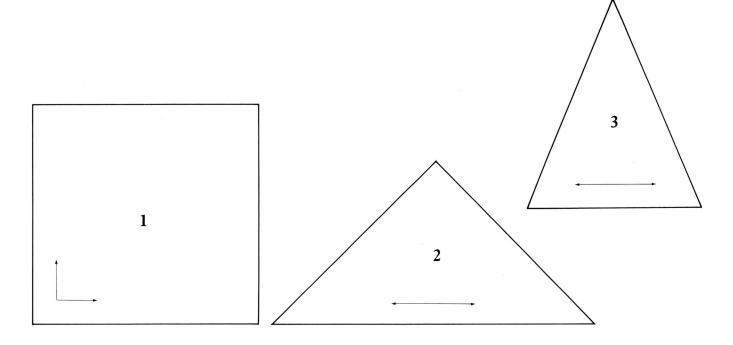

GOOSE TRACKS (1985) Pieced by Nancilu Burdick⋆

THE QUILT pictured here was patterned after Talula's late nineteenth-century *Goose Tracks* (*Legacy*, 13). The printed fabrics in the pieced blocks were gathered from quilt shops in at least ten Eastern states while I traveled to research the story of Talula and her quilts. Making it fulfilled my desire to create, as Talula did, a consistent and unified design from a great variety of small prints. The narrow strips that form the "cross in the center," the "framing" of the block and the 10½-inch block pattern, distinguish this from the majority of *Goose Tracks* printed patterns and suggest that Talula's quilt may have come from a pattern exchanged between nineteenth-century country women in central Georgia, where several similar quilts have been found.

In making such quilts from chosen fabrics rather than scraps from other projects, we are presented with difficult choices our grandmothers did not have to make. Their random selection of fabrics is difficult to imitate when we use newly bought fabrics or our own leftovers in scrap quilts.

Talula's sister, Nannie Gilbert Dickson, made an earlier *Goose Tracks*, not a scrap quilt, that was never quilted. The (c. 1870) date is indicated by its colors: red, green, and yellow-orange.[12] The quilt top was found with twenty-eight others in a lard can in the home of Nannie's granddaughter in Fayette County, Georgia, in 1989. Unlike Talula, who began to quilt her accumulated "nice quilts" in the 1890s as a release from suffering and heartache, Nannie left most of hers unquilted. More severely affected by her nightmarish memories of the Civil War and the grim realities of its aftermath, she was devastated by the deaths in her family. Beset by tragedies, she seemed unable in her later years to express her own creative abilities (*Legacy*, 121–124).

Detail of Nannie's Goose Tracks   (*Photo Courtesy John Lynch*)

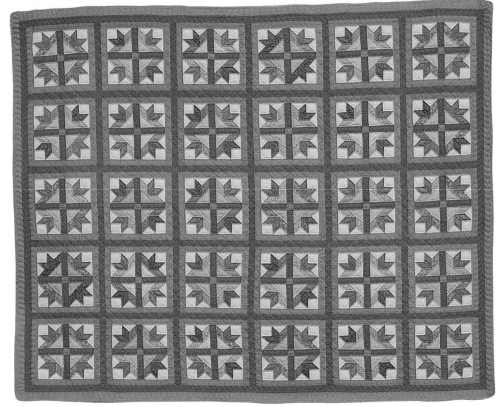

Goose Tracks   (*Burdick*)

Talula bordered a basic *Goose Tracks* block with one-and-one-half-inch strips, then joined them with one-and-one-half-inch sashing. The old-fashioned look is achieved by adding on a one-and-one-half- or two-inch border like the block strips to give the appearance of sashing extended to the outside edge. Block size: 11 inches.

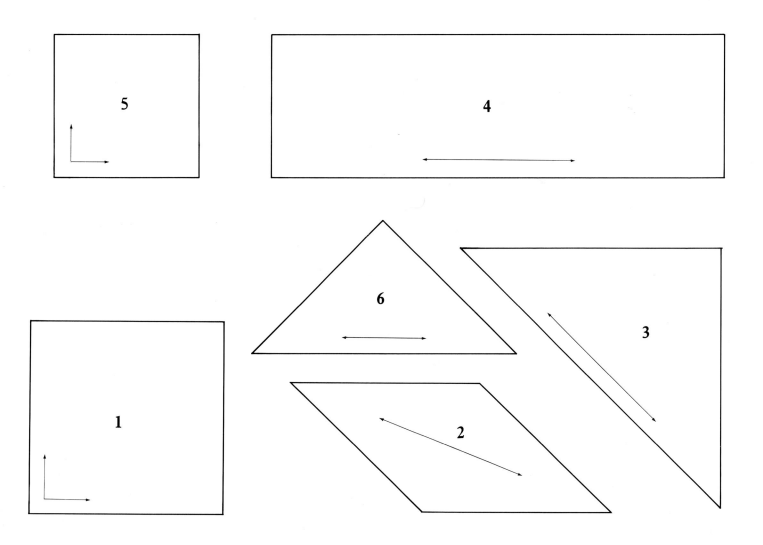

STAR AND CHAIN *(Ice Folly)* (1983) Michelle Fitch

TALULA CALLED her late-nineteenth-century quilt of this pattern *Star and Chain,* and though she did not think it beautiful, she saved it carefully until 1943. To have been so long treasured, the quilt must have held some special memories, but she did not consider it worth preserving as an heirloom. Before her death, therefore, she gave it to her son Burrell's family for everyday use (*Legacy,* 163). Made completely by hand (except for machine-applied binding) from assorted bold prints and unmatched pieces of white, the quilt reflects very hard times. Some of the white patches were cut from small scraps, themselves pieced, while the

backing was one piece of coarse, inexpensive "store-bought" muslin. Handed down through three generations after Talula's death, the quilt was hard used and often washed, yet still holds its bright colors to cheer a great grandson's family in Texas.

Michelle, who inherited a love of horses from her mother, has learned well the relationship of creativity to healing. She made her one-block wall hanging to memorialize a much loved and valued horse, Ice Folly, who had to be "put down." Her piece is yet another example of innumerable quilt projects undertaken as therapy to overcome grief or loss.

Ice Folly   *(Fitch)*

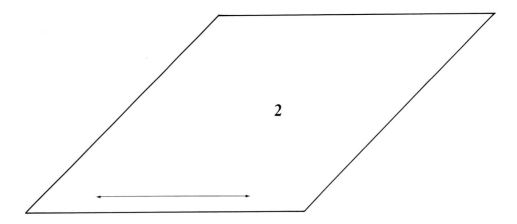

This is a basic *LeMoyne Star* with the "chain" created by adding on the diamond-and-triangle strip to the sides to make an octagon. Instead of using piece #3, Talula set her blocks together with twelve six-inch squares of muslin, fourteen half-squares, and four quarter squares (*Legacy*, 163). Such a setting creates other patterns where the "chain" seems to liberate the stars rather than confine them. Block size: 14 inches.

1

3

2

LITTLE SHOO-FLY (1987) Pieced by Nancilu Burdick*

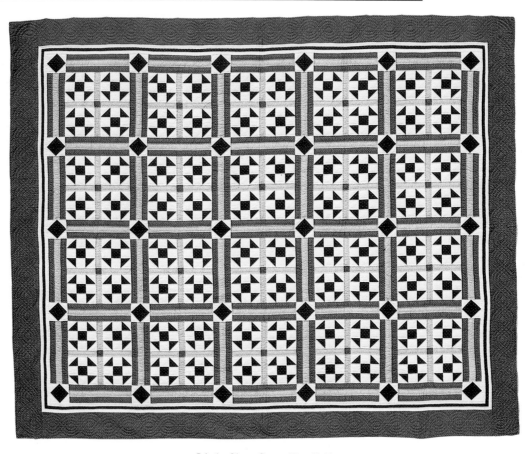

Little Shoo-fly   (*Burdick*)

WHAT IS THERE about an old handmade scrap quilt that preserves it as an object of continued and varied usefulness, generation after generation, until it is worn to shreds? One does not just cast away a quilt made by a beloved grandmother or aunt while descendants live who can find some use for it. Talula's once colorful and borderless *Shoo-Fly* (c. 1920) inspired the more formal one illustrated here. The old quilt has lost most of its color and much of its fabric, and even today one of Talula's granddaughters in the far West uses it as a dust cover for her washing machine and dryer, nearly seventy years later and three thousand miles from where it was made.

Making this new quilt to preserve the memory of Talula's *Shoo-Fly* was eminently satisfying, even though it required considerable time and patience. After the pieces were scissors-cut and the one-eighth-inch seams precisely marked, the hand-piecing was done over a two-year period while I traveled to research Talula's story. The inspiration for the colors of indigo blue and white came from the exhibit book *Homage to Amanda*, where seven "collectors' choice" quilts in this color-combination are shown.[13] At the suggestion of the collector, Gail Binney-Winslow, when I showed her my unquilted, borderless *Shoo-Fly* at the Huntsville Museum of Art in 1987, I decided to add the borders to this quilt.

Detail of Little Shoo-fly

Talula made a complex quilt from the simplest of nine-patch designs. The five-and-one-half-inch *Shoo-Fly* blocks are set together with one-inch strips to make a twelve-inch block. Twenty blocks can then be assembled with sashing and border to make an ample double bed quilt. Block size: 12 inches.

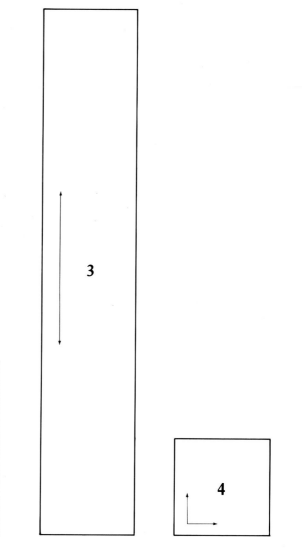

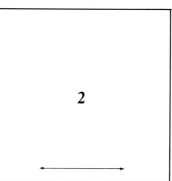

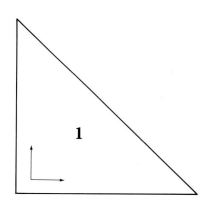

BEAR PAW (1991) Pieced by Nancilu Burdick

THE PATTERN for this popular design was first published by the Ladies Art Company in 1898. Here the pattern is drafted directly from a faded and worn quilt made by Talula in the 1930s. As was her custom, Talula made several *Bear Paw* quilts, and when World War II came on, one already quilted was donated to the Red Cross to help fund "Bundles for Britain." Another was given to Mrs. Gladie Coffman, a neighbor, in appreciation for managing an auction of four more of Talula's quilts to raise money for a community building. Upon its completion, Talula became an active member of the Oakdale Demonstration Club, continuing until she was eighty-four years old.

In December 1945, a news item under "Oakdale Community" appeared in the *Limestone County Democrat*. It congratulated Tom Bottoms on his eighty-fifth birthday and his wife Talula on being well enough to piece quilts again. Talula was eighty-four on February 15, 1946. She and Tom celebrated their sixty-third wedding anniversary on February 21, and two weeks later she passed quietly to her death. Talula had pieced her last quilt. Her final written words were found on a small piece of paper tucked into her well-worn Bible: "Your soul stood by me beckoning, my soul looked up for Joy."[14] She had asked Tom, who was keeping vigil by her bed, to lightly trace those words in pencil, so that even in her weakening condition she could follow them with her pen. In her own characteristic handwriting, she "spoke" her last testament of faith—in God and in her beloved husband. Only after Tom's death twenty months later did Almira find the note in her mother's Bible and realize its significance.

Detail of Bear Paw *(Burdick)*

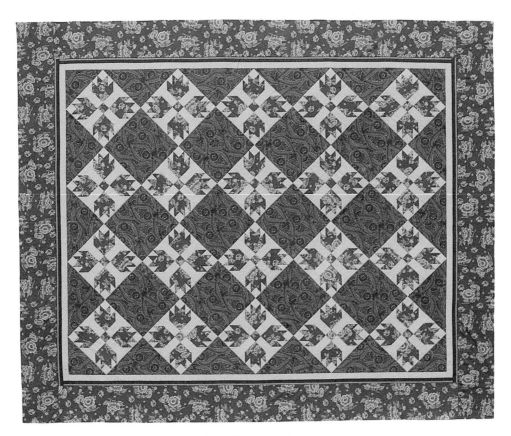

Unquilted Bear Paw

The small pieces in Talula's ten-inch pattern require precision in piecing and, therefore, careful marking of seams. Her original quilt was thirty blocks, made of multi-colored scraps and set together with two-and-one-half-inch Ely and Walker red-and-yellow calico. Block size: 10 inches.

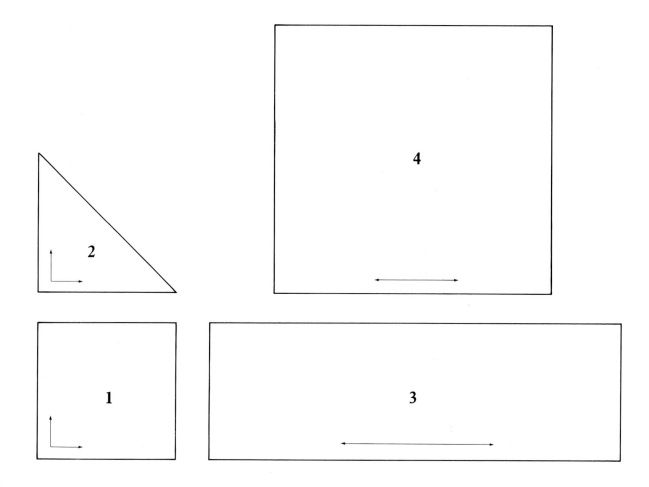

TREES IN THE PARK (c. 1925) Talula Gilbert Bottoms

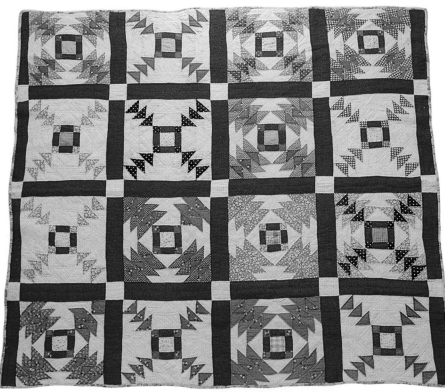

Trees in the Park   *(Bottoms)*

THIS PATTERN appeared in *Needlecraft* magazine in February 1934. Whether Talula ordered that pattern is not known, but she made this quilt sometime between 1920 and 1935 from scraps Almira saved for her, leftovers from her own four daughters' dresses. Eight siblings and numerous visiting cousins over the years used it for cover. It was considered "just an old scrap quilt," under which Almira's grandchildren were allowed to make tent playhouses long after Talula's death in 1946; and when Almira's third daughter, Mary, came home to the Southeast in 1975 from California, the *Trees in the Park* became "just any old quilt to keep me warm" in that first damp, cold winter in her Chattanooga apartment.[15] It remained in use until 1980. After nearly fifty years of giving comfort and warmth, it was put away at Almira's death to save for another generation.

The little flying bird prints in the center squares of the old quilt suggested *Trees in the Forest* as a name for this new version. Since no other quilt Talula made in this pattern has been found, the new quilt will preserve the memory of Talula's quilt when it is finally laid away for good.

Detail of Trees in the Park

Trees in the Forest   *(1990)   Pieced by Nancilu Burdick*★

Detail of Trees in the Forest   *(Burdick)*

This seemingly complex, sixty-five-piece block requires visualizing three separate units composed of smaller pieces, a rectangle and three sizes of triangles. First piece the central rectangle; it is the horizontal bar of a "fat cross." Add a triangle (#2) to each end of this rectangle to complete the first unit. Piece a larger triangle (from #1 and #2 triangles) and add to top and bottom of the first unit to make a square. Finally piece the four corner triangles and add on to complete the block. This procedure requires stitching only straight seams, and the pattern is then executed with ease.

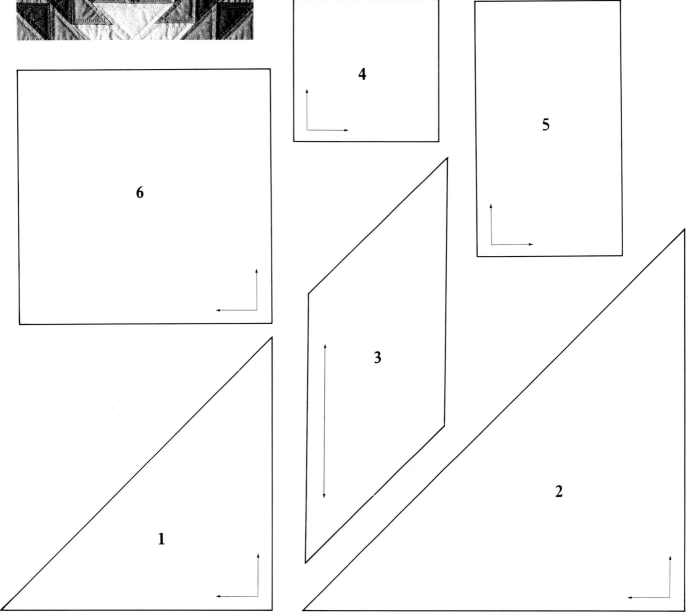

IMPROVED NINE-PATCH (c. 1941) Talula Gilbert Bottoms

THE QUILT pictured here is one Talula made in her later years, perhaps as late as 1943 or 1944. The pattern is similar to one that appeared in the *Kansas City Star* in 1933, and Talula found it easy to piece by hand, its curved patches notwithstanding. She made "one for each of the children" in shades of white, green, blue, and aqua, leaving most of them for others to quilt. Both pattern and fabrics may have been sent to her by her unmarried daughter Mollie Ruth, a college teacher in Oklahoma, who saved her mother's letters:

> *Many, many* thanks for the prints. They are so pretty. You may go to the store and get 5 or 6 yards more of the green, for I may make several of those quilts when I get started. . . . Tell the ladie I thank her very much for the square and patterns. . . .[16]

Six of Talula's *Improved Nine-Patch* quilts, each made with one solid and one print fabric, remain in like-new condition with her descendants. The green and white one shown here was given to Mollie Ruth after it was quilted by Mrs. Brewer, a Limestone County woman who was known for her "nice quilting" and who charged five dollars for her best work in the 1940s.

Quite appropriately, Talula Bottoms and Lucy May Brewer, who together produced innumerable quilts that survive today, are buried almost side by side in the Bottoms Cemetery near Athens, Alabama. Mrs. Brewer lived to be ninety-one and died in 1964.

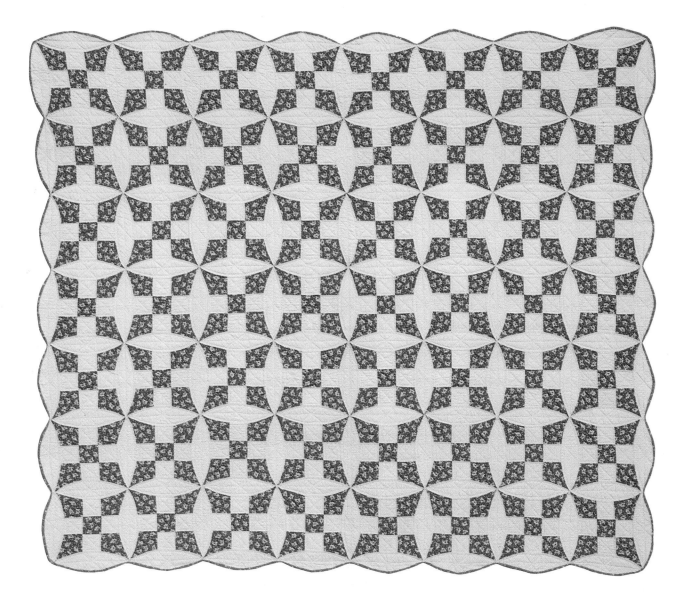

Improved Nine-Patch   *(c. 1941)*   *Talula Gilbert Bottoms*

Improved Nine-Patch   *(1988)   Nancilu Burdick*★

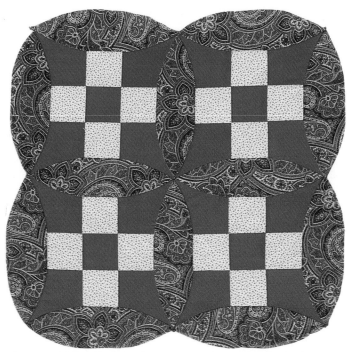

Improved Nine-Patch   *(in process 1990)   Michelle Fitch*

This quilt is pieced and assembled just as any of the simpler *Nine-Patch* patterns. Where the melon-shaped pieces come together (to form the sashing), care must be taken to stitch just to the end of the marked seams. Eight points come together here (as in a *LeMoyne Star*), and they must match precisely. Block size: 15½ inches, including sash.

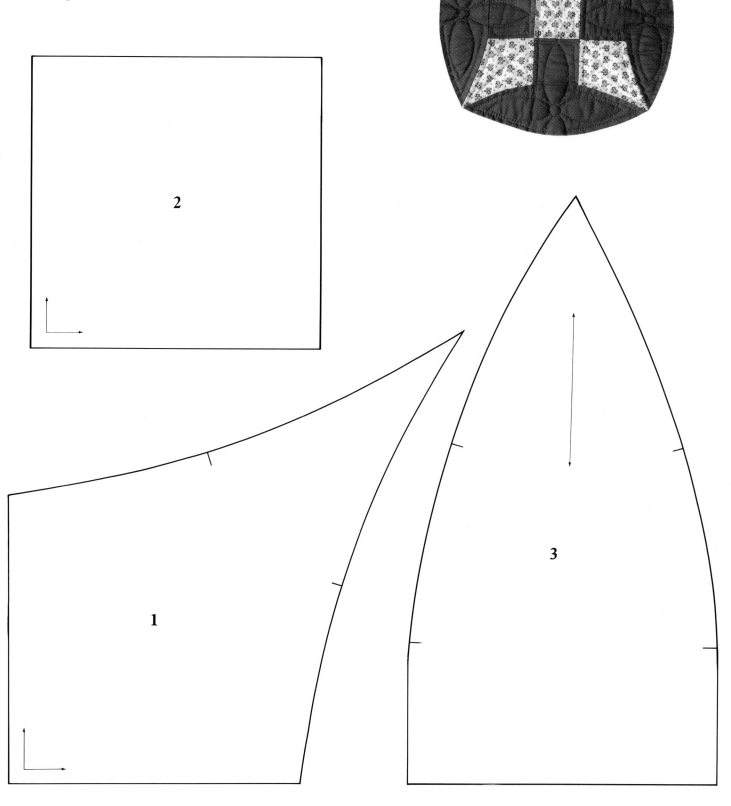

AROUND THE WORLD (c. 1941–1945) Pieced by Talula Gilbert Bottoms,
assembled by Almira Butler (1950), quilted by Nancilu Burdick (1990–1991)

ON MAY 17, 1941, Talula wrote to her daughter Mollie Ruth that she had begun "a new quilt that Papa likes so much he wants to find someone to quilt it and he keep it. It is real pretty, although it is just a scrap quilt. Name of it is Around the World."[17]

Nations "around the world" were engaged in a massive war, the United States had already begun conscription, and five of Tom and Talula's grandsons would soon be called to fight. While "Papa" listened intently to every alarming newscast, Talula's hands worked skillfully to create order from a scrap bag of bold patterned prints, some of them dotted and splashed with red like drops of blood. Almost fifty years later, her granddaughter would be quilting the final stitches on one of those quilts, just as the air waves around the world vibrated with the alarms of yet another war.

Talula finished piecing her first *Around the World* quilt in less than two weeks. Despite the chaos and tragedy of war, she serenely went on to make "one for each of the children," six in all. To have them quilted, she had to "get Burlie to take me up in Tennessee to find Mrs. Brewer—since her husband died she has moved up there to live near her children." Talula found such satisfaction in using up her scraps that she continued to piece *Around the World* blocks as long as she lived, and made enough for six or eight more quilts. She filled in the background with solid yellow, blue, or green, and left them for others to assemble and quilt.

The old quilt pictured here was one of the twenty-five or more quilt tops assembled by daughter Almira from blocks pieced in the 1940s by Talula. I added the borders and completed the quilting in January 1991. The Old Chelsea Station Needlework Service pattern appeared in the *Kansas City Star* in 1940, though Talula may have had it from another source.

Talula's *Around the World* pattern with its little fan blocks forming a circle around the cross invited more than replication; it seems to ask us to find our own way in a world far different from

Around the World Variation   *(1991)*   *Nancilu Burdick★*

our grandmothers'. For this variation I made twelve additional fans and experimented by placing them in different positions around the basic block. I wanted to create a shifting pattern and contain the rhythm with the illusion of sashing. This I accomplished by setting together six eighteen-inch blocks, ten half-blocks, and four quarter-blocks. Other designs will result by re-arranging the twelve fan blocks around the central *Around the World* block.

This pattern, with its curved patches, can be pieced more easily and accurately by hand than by machine. It is essential to mark the seam lines carefully and to stitch only on the marked lines just to the seam allowances.

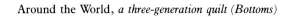

Around the World, *a three-generation quilt (Bottoms)*

The curved patches make this a bit more complex to piece, and pin-basting is absolutely necessary. Seams need to be marked and stitched precisely. Care must be taken to match the diminishing points at the outer "fan" edges (when assembling the blocks contiguously) to create the concave diamond shapes, as in Talula's quilt, or other variations such as the medallions in mine. Basic block size: 10 inches.

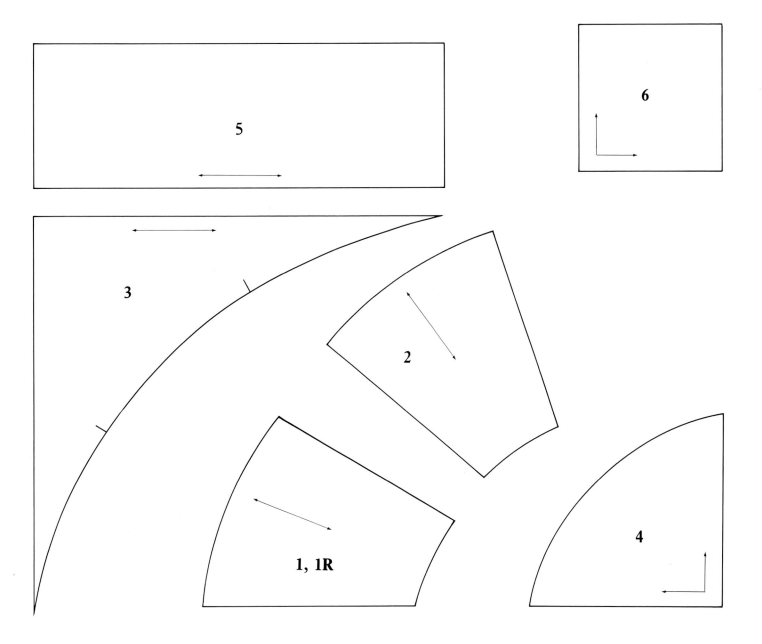

QUEEN OF THE MAY (c. 1920) Talula Gilbert Bottoms

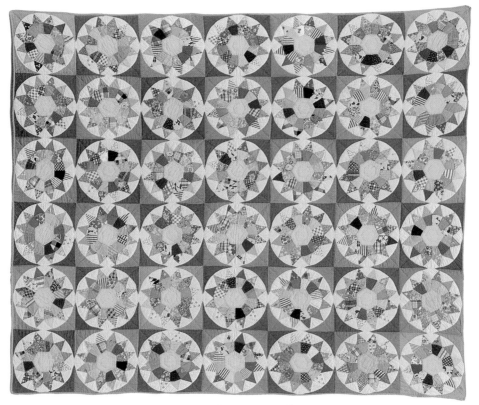

Queen of the May   *(Bottoms)*

THIS PATTERN, first published by Old Chelsea Station Needlework Service, New York, appeared later as a Laura Wheeler design in *Needlecraft* magazine. Talula made at least three *Queen of the May* quilts between 1910 and 1930, varying the background colors while using up accumulated scraps. The quilts were found with her grandchildren in Michigan, New York state, and finally Nevada, where this one was first photographed in 1986.

Talula pieced and assembled her quilt entirely by hand. The quilting "in the ditch" and machine binding with purchased bias tape suggest it was completed by someone else. The pattern is another example of curved-patch piecing, easily done by hand for an experienced quilter, and a favorite with Talula. Dorothy has chosen to piece the twelve-point star circle and appliqué it to a larger background block.

Queen of the May   *(1989)   Dorothy Frost*

This pattern with its curved patches becomes easier after piecing a block or two. Join a light and dark piece and attach (by twos) to each side of the hexagon to form the inner circle. Join the light and dark triangles alternately and add on, a half circle at a time. Finally, attach the corner pieces to complete the square. Block size: 12 inches.

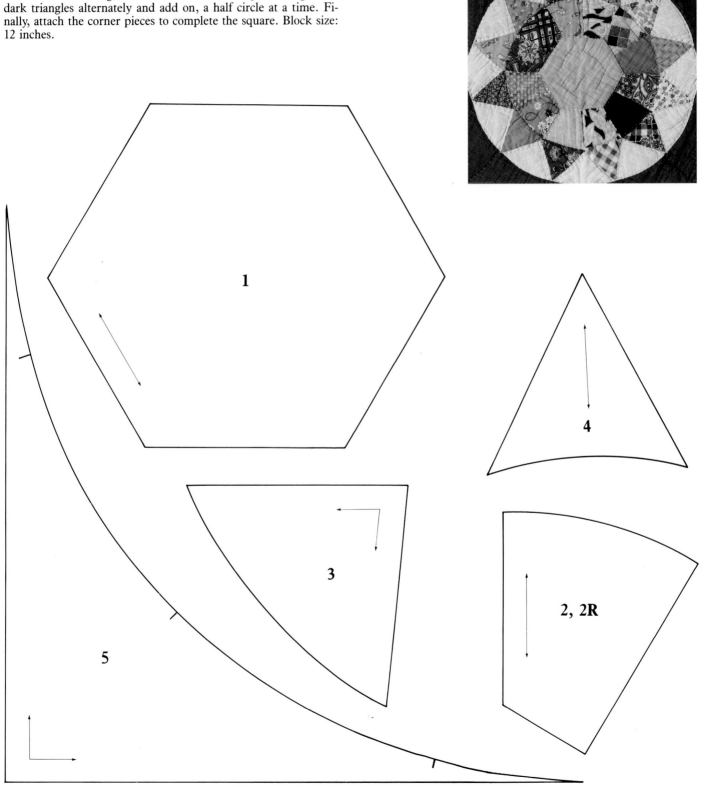

GRECIAN STAR (c. 1940) Talula Gilbert Bottoms

Grecian Star   (*Bottoms*)

AMONG TALULA's saved letters from family and friends are several thanking her for the "beautiful quilt." Apparently she sent quilts as expressions of love and sympathy much as we send greeting cards today. Four *Grecian Star* quilts sent as such gifts have been found. The seventeen-inch block design was one she could piece with longer stitches and wider seams and assemble in about one week, despite failing eyesight and crippled hands. In her later years she laid away stacks of *Grecian Star* quilt tops as well as other designs in her trunk for gift-giving occasions, and eventually most of her grandchildren had one. Talula apparently ordered the pattern from W. L. M. Clark, Inc., St. Louis, Missouri. Her handwritten note to her daughter Almira, "This is like the 3 I have made for you folks," appears beside that pattern in the company's pattern booklet, *Grandmother's Patchwork Quilt Designs*, Book 20, 1934, found in Talula's pattern collection.

The old quilt pictured here was discovered in 1990 in Tennessee. Talula and Tom had made the trip in the early 1940s to find their niece, Essie Bottoms Konig, "to see her fine family," and to present her the quilt. Essie quilted it herself, and at her death she left it to her unmarried daughters Mildred and Bessie, along with two older quilts, one made by their grandmother Laura Ann Collins Bottoms and the other by their great-grandmother Eliza McElroy Bottoms. Mildred and Bessie continue the quiltmaking tradition themselves, and until recently they also operated their own quilt and fabric shop.

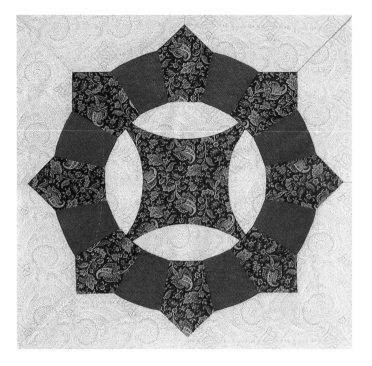

Grecian Star   (*1990*)   *Michelle Fitch*

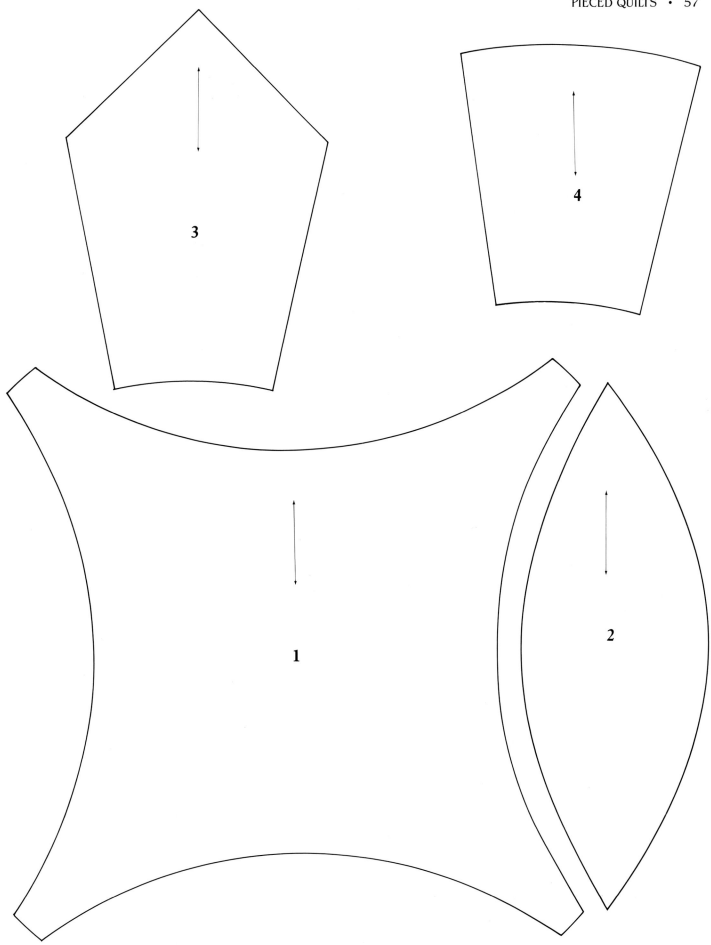

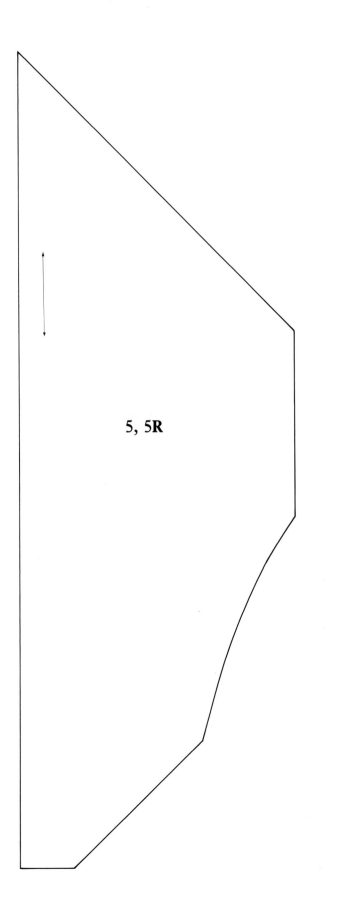

5, 5R

This pattern is best made from the inside out, the melon-shaped pieces added to the "reel" to make a circular center, which is pieced into the star. The four corners are then pieced and joined to the star and the seams finally closed at the sides. Block size: 17 inches.

SUNFLOWER (1990) Barbara Nagel

SUNFLOWER, AROUND the World, Grecian Star and *Improved Nine-Patch:* all were quilt designs Talula continued to piece into her eighties. Grandchildren were getting married, and she wanted to make quilts for them. When a grandchild stopped by to see her and admired a quilt in process, she more often than not went to her trunk, took out a finished top like it, and said, "Honey, you just take this one."

When the United States entered World War II, Talula knew she might have to face the sacrifice of grandsons in this, the third major war she was about to witness. Nonetheless, at eighty, when citizens were asked to do their part, she would work with as much speed and patriotic fervor as anyone, making quilt after quilt to be auctioned by the Red Cross.

The *Sunflower,* a pattern she could piece and assemble quickly, was one such quilt. As articles about this unusual octogenarian appeared in the local paper in 1943, Talula clipped and sent them to her daughter, Mollie Ruth.

Does Her Part.

Mrs. T. J. Bottoms, better known as "Grandmother Bottoms" of Oakdale Club in Limestone county who has celebrated her 60th anniversary is finding plenty she can do to help the war effort. She has already pieced four quilts for the Red Cross and helped with two Bundles for Britain.

Even though she keeps busy doing her own cooking she finds time to help in community betterment. Four other quilts are completed to be sold to help on a community building. . . .[18]

How many *Sunflowers* Talula made can only be estimated. A dozen have been found, many hard used and badly worn, some like new, and several in unquilted tops. The pattern, not found in the usual printed pattern sources of that time, may have been sent to her by a Texas relative from whom she saved many letters[19] (*Legacy,* 157).

Sunflower   (*Nagel*)

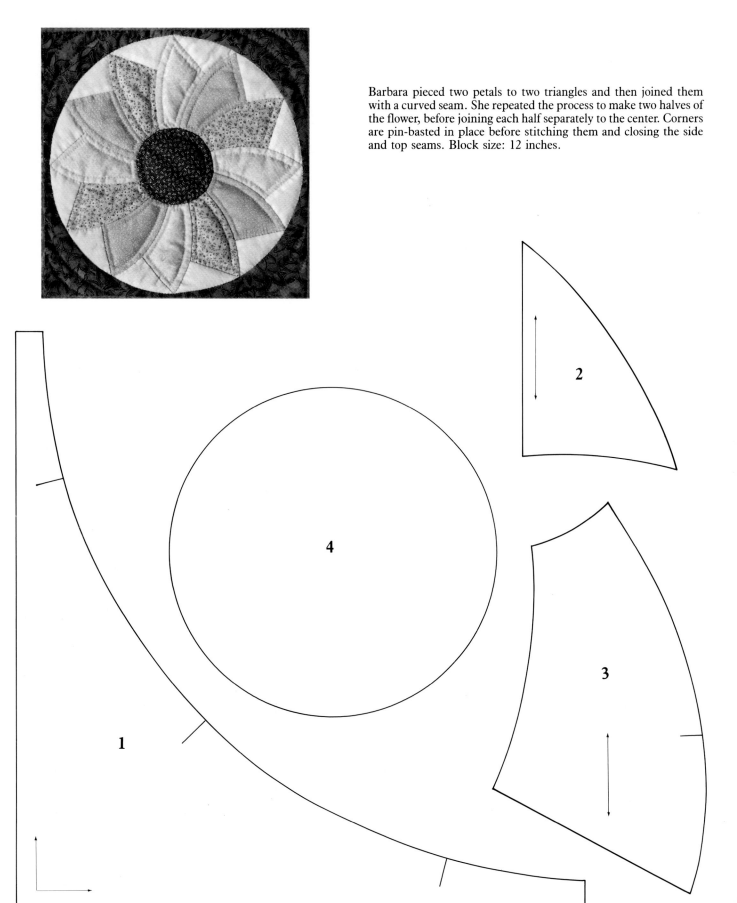

Barbara pieced two petals to two triangles and then joined them with a curved seam. She repeated the process to make two halves of the flower, before joining each half separately to the center. Corners are pin-basted in place before stitching them and closing the side and top seams. Block size: 12 inches.

2

4

3

1

GLITTERING STAR (1990) Barbara Nagel

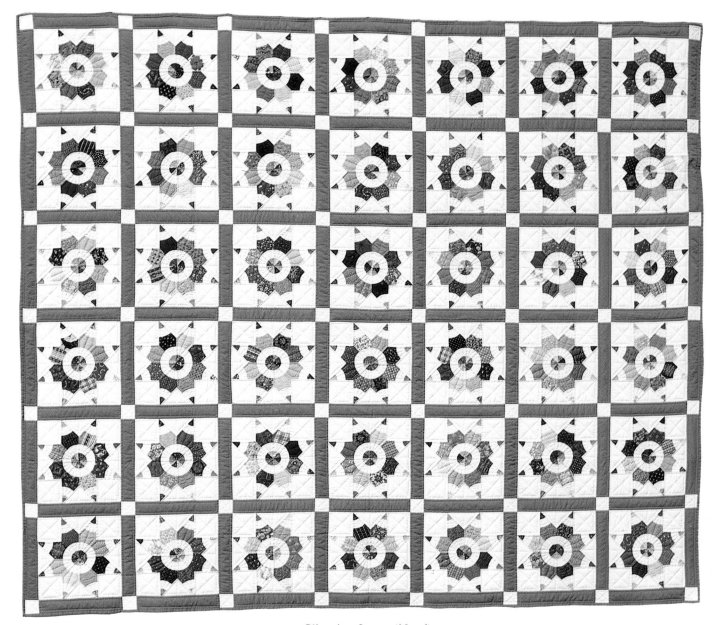

Glittering Star   *(Nagel)*

OF ALL TALULA's pieced patterns, the one she called *Glittering Star* seems to have been made over the longest period and survived in the best condition in the greatest numbers. Eight finished quilts and one unquilted top of this design, made between 1890 and 1940, remain with descendants (*Legacy*, 148, 152–53). The unfinished quilt reveals Talula's characteristic unmarked, one-eighth-inch seams evenly hand-stitched, and almost perfect matching of the pattern pieces. Its twenty blocks are assembled with a wide pieced sashing of Ely and Walker calicoes and joined at corners with matching nine-patch blocks. It appears to have been made in the 1920s or 1930s at the peak of Talula's productivity.

A like design called *Queen's Star* was published by Aunt Martha Studios (The Colonial Pattern Company) in the early 1930s, long after the old pattern's origin.

Barbara Nagel was fascinated by the design and chose solid blue sashing to assemble her forty-two-block quilt, more like a replica of Talula's 1930s work. Barbara, a one-stitch-at-a-time quilter, cut, pieced, assembled, quilted, and bound her quilt by hand, completing it in just nine months. Without conscious intention, for she had not imposed that significant time limit on herself, she created the quilt quite naturally and with a sense of fulfillment very like motherhood.

Detail of Glittering Star *(Nagel)*

Glittering Star *(c. 1930) Talula Gilbert Bottoms (Photography by Jennifer)*

This is a rather elegant variation of a "string-pieced" *LeMoyne Star.* The light and dark "scraps" are arranged to form the eight diamonds, with concentric center circles and "glittering" dark points. Careful marking of seams is essential. Block size: 12 inches.

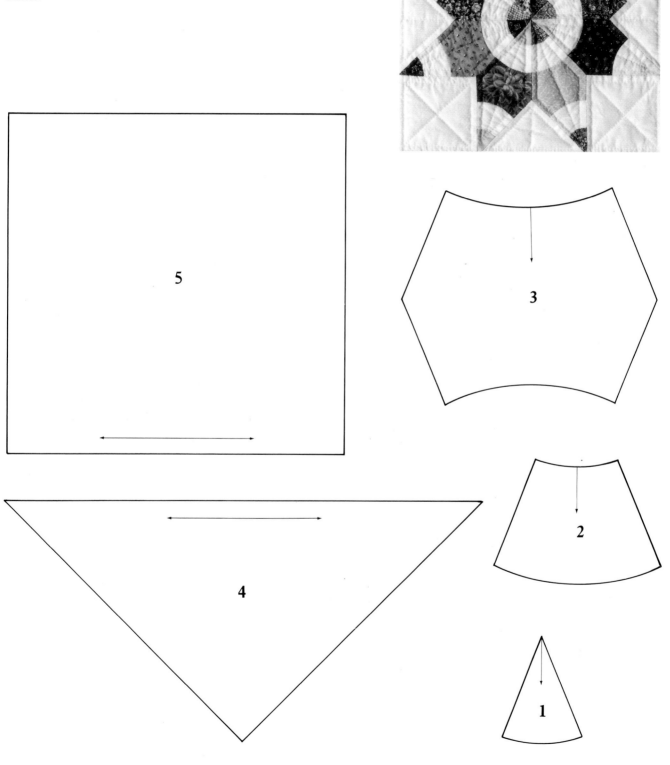

INDIAN WEDDING RING (c. 1890) Talula Gilbert Bottoms

ONE OF THE MOST exciting aspects of family quilt research is the discovery of a long-sought quilt, one that has proved so elusive that it is given up for lost. Such was the case with "a most unusual *Wedding Ring* quilt that won first place as an antique quilt in the county fair." This observation had come from two of Talula's grandchildren in 1985.[20] Their mother, Nettie Goodwin Bottoms, Talula's daughter-in-law—career teacher, skilled horsewoman, and a fine quilter herself—had inherited much of Talula's unfinished work and some of her most cherished quilts.

Before Nettie Bottoms gave the *Indian Wedding Ring* to her only son, she entered it in a county fair, perhaps Jefferson County, New York, where for many years her husband, Talula's son Emmett, was a revered minister. It won first place in the antique category there.

It was not until fall 1989 that I discovered the *Indian Wedding Ring,* as well as two other quilts made by Talula, in a small New York state town with Nettie and Emmett Bottoms' granddaughter. Although often washed, it is well preserved; the hand-piecing of the entire top, the close double-line quilting, and the hand-applied narrow binding top-stitched by machine are characteristic of the work of skilled nineteenth-century quilters in the Southeast. Mystery still accompanies the old quilt, however, for the teal blue and light brown colors are unlike the colors in other quilts made by Talula before the turn of the century. Is it possible that the original colors were red and green? The one small square rather than four patches connecting the melon-shaped pieces and the relatively small size of the rings mark this as an unusual *Indian Wedding Ring* pattern.[21]

Two patterns are given here: a thirteen-inch one like Talula's, and a ten-inch block suitable for a smaller piece such as the one illustrated below.

Indian Wedding Ring   *(1990)*   *Barbara Nagel*

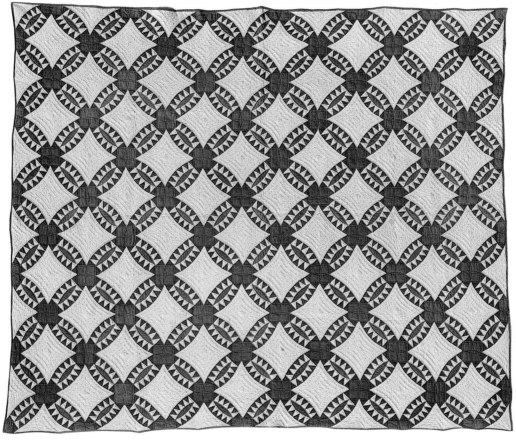

Indian Wedding Ring   (c. *1890?*)   *Talula Gilbert Bottoms*

Detail of Indian Wedding Ring   *(Nagel)*

Once the pieced sides of each of the melon shapes that form the interlocking "rings" are made, the quilt is assembled with relative ease, either diagonally as in Talula's quilt or horizontally as in Barbara's wall piece. Talula's quilt uses long, diagonal strips of the sawtooth melons, joined with the small squares as a kind of sashing for the rest of the sawtooth melons, which are set alternately with the concave squares form strips from corner to corner. Barbara has made four rings and set them together with the center and outside to concave shapes. Two block sizes: 10½ inches and 13 inches.

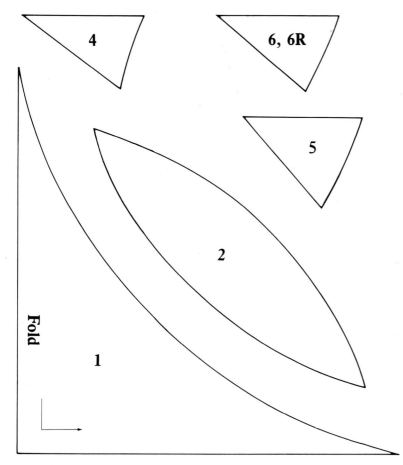

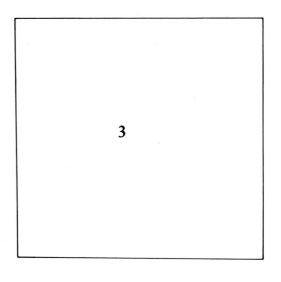

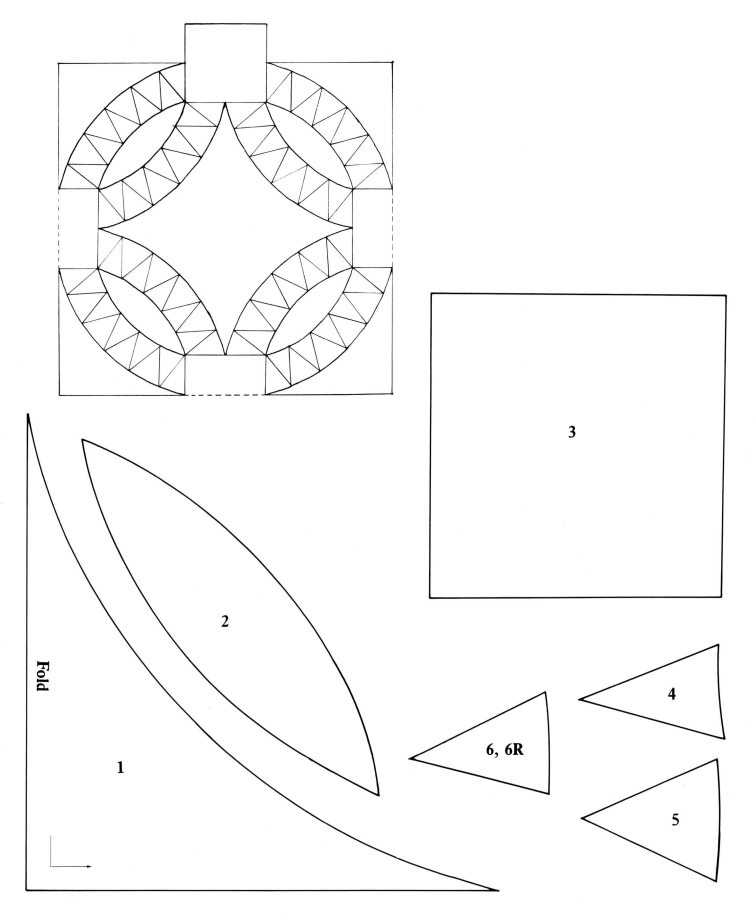

Fold

1

2

3

4

5

6, 6R

LIFEBOAT (1990) Fay Joerg

Lifeboat   (*Joerg*)

TALULA's *LIFEBOAT* has a detailed history recorded in letters she wrote to her children in 1934 and 1935, in particular to her daughter Mollie Ruth, for whom she made the quilt.[22] The quilt and Talula's name for it reflect her circumstances during the Great Depression and her characteristic approach to her life's difficulties (*Legacy*, 140–141). Talula drafted the difficult pieced pattern in 1934 directly from "the old quilt of my mother's that went to Bud." Talula saved the brown paper patterns, as well as a single, unquilted block she made, either as a trial block or as an example for a daughter-in-law who planned to make a *Lifeboat*, to show how the design was to be put together.[23]

Completing this quilt was like a rebirth for Talula, for in it she returned to her nineteenth-century standards, proving she was still capable of executing intricate piecework and doing exquisite quilting. In the face of hard times and heartbreak, she seemed rejuvenated to a measure of creativity that for the next ten years enabled her to produce quilts at an astonishing rate.

The origin of this very old quilt design, like most old patterns, is lost in time. Named *Whig's Defeat*—possibly in 1844 when Henry Clay, a Whig, was defeated by James K. Polk—it was earlier called the *Democrat*.[24] It was popular in the Piedmont area of North Carolina, from whence Talula's maternal grandparents had migrated in the 1820s. The custom of setting the blocks together without sashing, as Talula did, and accenting them with rose-cross appliqué, seems also to have been a common practice there.[25]

Holly Gilbert's design, with its pieced diamonds, triangles, and curved patches, is for experienced quilters. The pattern here offers variously shaped diamonds and triangles to result in a neatly fitting, flat design. Women of Holly's and Talula's generations would not have been so precise because they knew they could ease in fullness to fit a curved patch and their quilting would take up any excess. They were not so obsessed with technical perfection in piecing as with the overall beauty of the finished quilt.

Lifeboat   (c. 1935)   *Talula Gilbert Bottoms*   (*Photography by Jennifer*)

Lifeboat   (1990)   *Fay Joerg*

Detail of Lifeboat   (*Bottoms*)

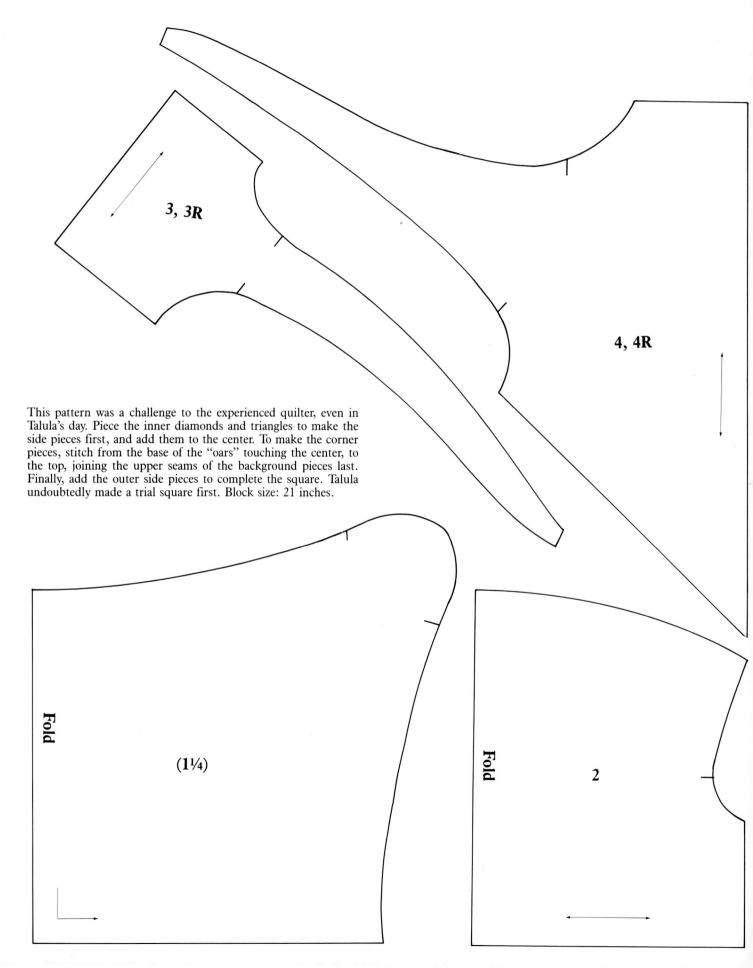

This pattern was a challenge to the experienced quilter, even in Talula's day. Piece the inner diamonds and triangles to make the side pieces first, and add them to the center. To make the corner pieces, stitch from the base of the "oars" touching the center, to the top, joining the upper seams of the background pieces last. Finally, add the outer side pieces to complete the square. Talula undoubtedly made a trial square first. Block size: 21 inches.

3, 3R

4, 4R

Fold

(1¼)

Fold

2

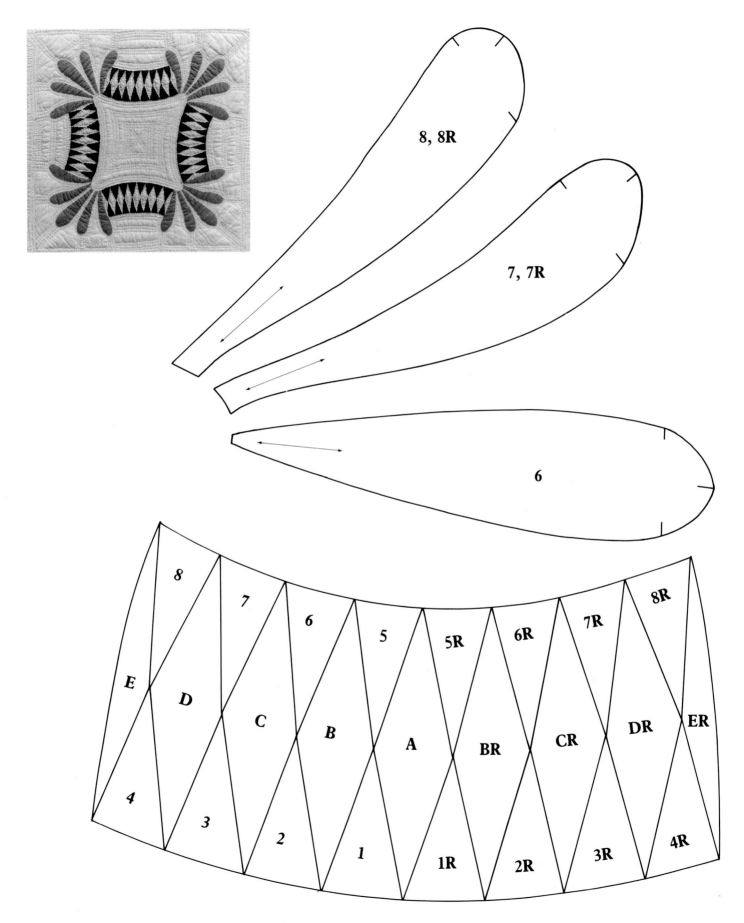

8, 8R

7, 7R

6

8

7

6

5

5R

6R

7R

8R

E

D

C

B

A

BR

CR

DR

ER

4

3

2

1

1R

2R

3R

4R

QUEEN'S PARASOL (1990) Barbara Nagel

THE PATTERN pieces for this unusual Aunt Martha design were drafted directly from Talula's 8½ x 11-inch pattern sheet found among her collection with the much-perforated tissue paper shapes she used to cut the patches. The quilt she made from the pattern has so far eluded discovery.

The seam allowance on Talula's *Queen's Parasol* pattern was one-eighth inch, rather than the usual one-fourth inch, which permitted accurate hand-piecing of the curved patches without marking seams, a time-consuming procedure she never practiced.

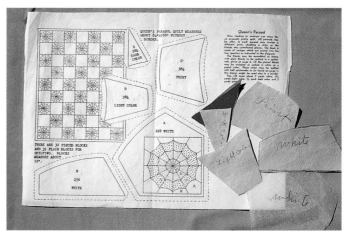

Photograph of Talula's Queen's Parasol *pattern leaflet and patterns*

Queen's Parasol   (*Nagel*)

Queen's Parasol *block*   (*1990*)
Nancilu Burdick

Marking of seams is suggested for quilters whose eyes and fingers have been trained to use seam-line marking. One-eight- or three-sixteenth-inch seam allowances are recommended for easing together the twelve center points. The pattern is more easily put together if it is first worked in wedges, which are then joined into quarters and pieced as a four-patch block. Block size: 12 inches.

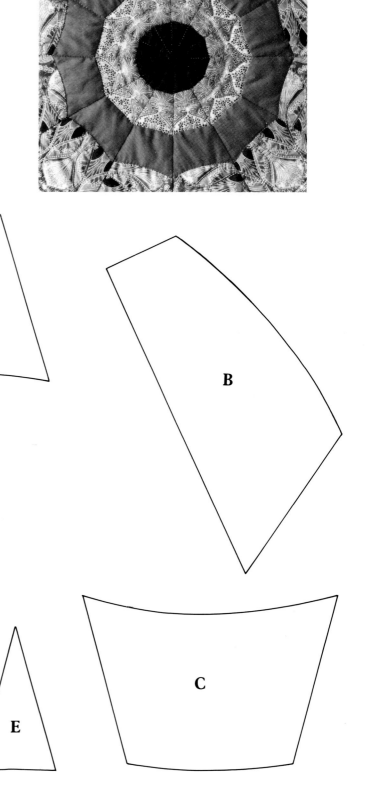

D

B

A

E

C

FULL BLOWN TULIP detail (c. 1910)   Talula Gilbert Bottoms

TALULA'S C. 1910 QUILT WAS my inspiration for a *Sampler* quilt I made of thirty various blocks pieced and assembled in a six-session learn-to-quilt class. After hand-piecing three quilts in 1984, teaching myself as my hands grew accustomed to using the long-neglected needle, I had realized I needed instruction if I was ever to progress in what I felt urged to do, to replicate a number of Talula's quilts that charmed me (and belonged to others), in order to feel sufficiently connected with my grandmother to write her story.

In fact, it took a catastrophic accident, involving a spinal injury and the threat of paralysis, to turn my life around and face me toward the craftsmanship that released my "writers' block" and enabled me to pursue the work I felt honor-bound to complete (*Legacy*, 7–11). In making the *Sampler* quilt largely by hand, I learned the therapeutic value of hand sewing. Its completion did indeed allow me to realize a closer connection with both my talented grandmother and my own neglected potential.

Talula's *Full Blown Tulip* with its fifty-six blocks was made by a pattern first printed in the Ladies Art Company 1898 catalog (*Legacy*, 114). Filled with her own thick hand-carded cotton from the Cullman County farm, its tiny quilting stitches are evidence of a skilled, efficient woman who never wasted a "moment, a motion, or a thing." Her responsibilities were legion at the time, her health failing, and money for cloth so scarce it came only from her own efforts—marketing her prize flocks of chickens and ducks, selling or bartering with their eggs and with butter from cows she tended and milked herself. All this while she still cooked for her children and husband, did the usual heavy house and garden work, canned and preserved on a wood stove, washed clothing outdoors summer and winter with a "rub board" and a "battling block" with water heated by a wood fire under a black cast-iron pot, and ironed with heavy flatirons.

When did she have time and space to move furniture, put her big quilting frame on chair backs, and quilt this and numerous other quilts? It seems impossible. But it did happen with innumerable women of her generation and circumstances; *making* time for creative work was their own quiet liberation from feeling oppressed in their role as women. This kind of resourcefulness and efficiency is our heritage, to nurture and express in our own times and circumstances and pass on to future generations.

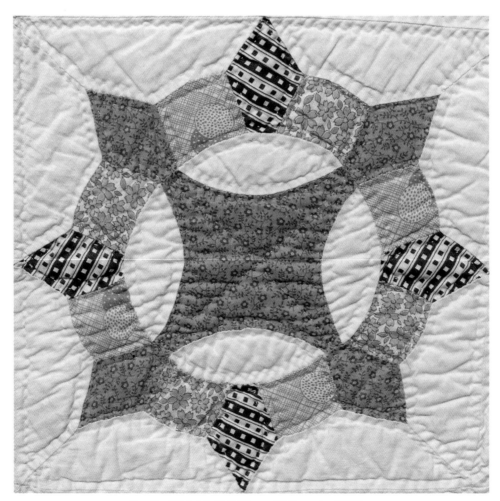

Detail of Talula's Full Blown Tulip   *(c. 1910)*

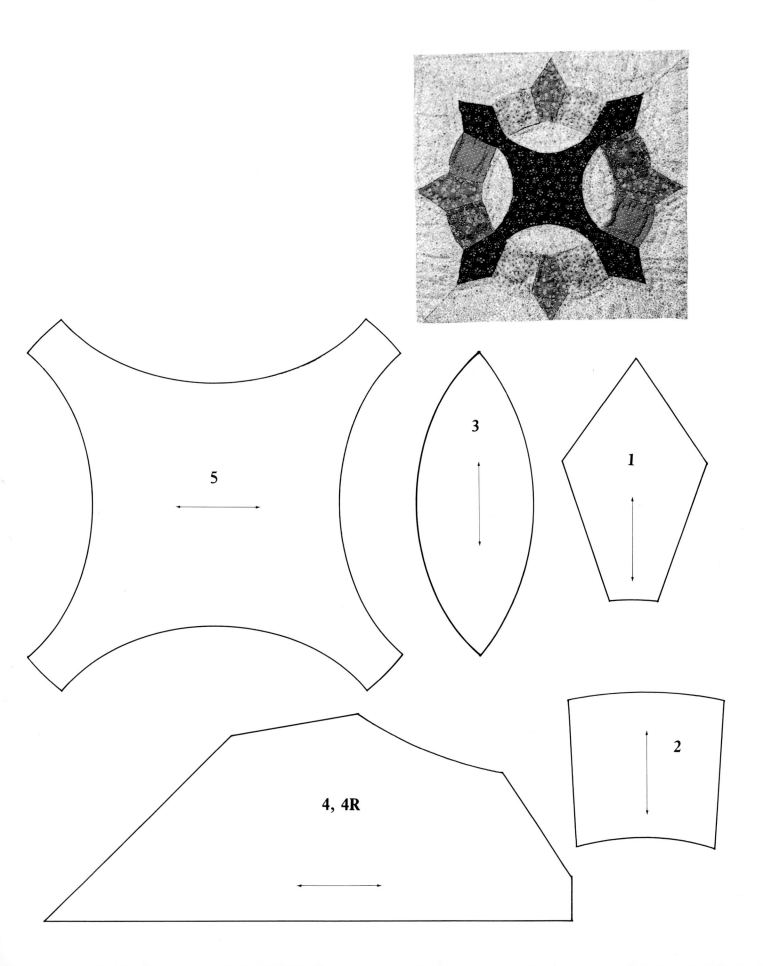

5

3

1

2

4, 4R

This pattern is a bit more complex than the *Grecian Star*, but relatively easy to piece once you've mastered the smaller curved patches. Add on corner pieces the same as for *Grecian Star* (pages 56–58). Block size: 11 inches.

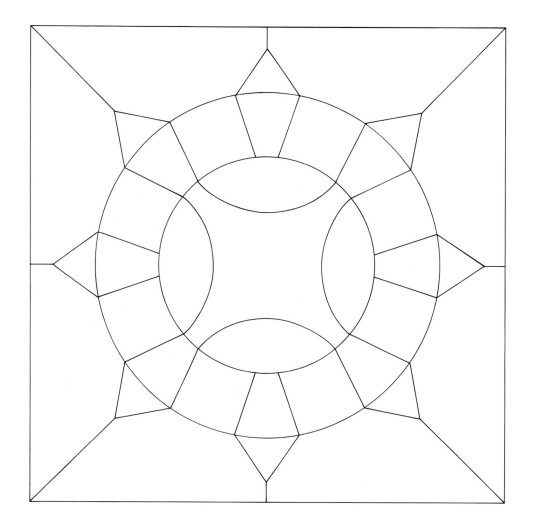

PART II

*P*IECED AND *A*PPLIQUÉ *Q*UILTS

Detail of Orange Bud *(1989) Michelle Fitch*

PIECED AND APPLIQUÉ QUILTS

*C*ombining pieced designs with appliqué is a very old tradition, so ancient that its origins cannot be traced. The earliest known example is said to be an Egyptian queen's funeral canopy from 980 B.C., pieced of dyed gazelle leather and appliquéd with symbolic figures and the sacred lotus blossom.[1] It is in the Museum of Cairo in Egypt. How many quilters would be astonished to realize, when they use this combination, that they are continuing a tradition nearly three thousand years old.

Innumerable examples of nineteenth-century quilts remain, many illustrating a combination of pieced work and appliqué. It is interesting to discover that two of the oldest known American patchwork quilts existing today are also examples of appliqué. Anna Tuel's wedding quilt (1785) and Mary Johnson's 1793 quilt both undoubtedly were made with special care and new materials.[2] At the other end of the spectrum and just as inspiring are folk quilts, some of them made from remnants and salvaged pieces of old clothes, but

nevertheless showing a high degree of skill and imagination in the use of symbols and representational figures. The Harriet Powers Bible quilt (1886) now at the Smithsonian Institution,[3] and the Haskins Family quilt (1870) at the Shelbourne Museum in Vermont[4] are examples of the humbler type. Talula Bottoms' *Bluebirds* Depression quilt, with its pieced crazy-patch setting blocks and appliquéd "bluebirds of happiness," though not as original perhaps, demonstrates sensitive imagination, love, and resourcefulness. Such quilts show that a need for symbolic expression of emotions, truths, and native talents is not the exclusive domain of trained artists.

The seven patterns in this section range from the simplicity of the half-pieced, half-appliquéd *Tulip Basket* to the more complex, almost wholly pieced *Orange Bud*, with only its stem appliquéd. All together they are a fair representation of the versatility of Talula's work.

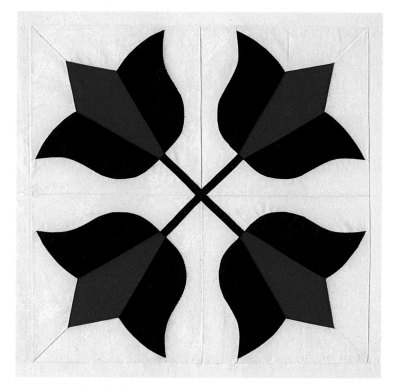

Detail of Dutch Tulip   *(1990)   Michelle Fitch*

TULIP BASKET (1990) Dorothy Frost

Tulip Basket (*Frost*)

TALULA MADE two quilts in this design, one for each daughter, and set the blocks on the diagonal with alternate plain muslin blocks. Both have the pieced Greek Key border she used in the six *Garden Bouquet* quilts (*Legacy,* 144), and in both the deeper blues have proved unstable after washing and extended exposure to light. They were quilted in a simple diamond background pattern, just as Talula's first *Garden Bouquet* was. These similarities suggest that the quilts may have been made from a Nancy Page (Florence LaGanke) design that Talula clipped from the *Nashville Banner* in the early 1930s.

The large blocks and appliqué pieces and the simplicity of the pieced basket triangle result in a pattern that is easy to assemble in a short time.

General Instructions

The appliqué designs in the following patterns do not require the precision essential for the pieced portions. After both sections are completed, as in the *Tulip Basket*, *Pear Basket* and *Dutch Tulip*, sew the two triangles together, hiding the stems of the tulips inside the seams.

Detail of Tulip Basket (*c. 1935*) *Talula Gilbert Bottoms*

For this easy pattern, make the two triangles, one pieced and one appliqué, and join them together to hide the stems. Twelve blocks, set on point with alternating plain squares, make a double quilt. Talula's was finished with a Greek Key border made with 2-inch contrasting strips. (*Legacy*, p. 144) Block size: 14 inches.

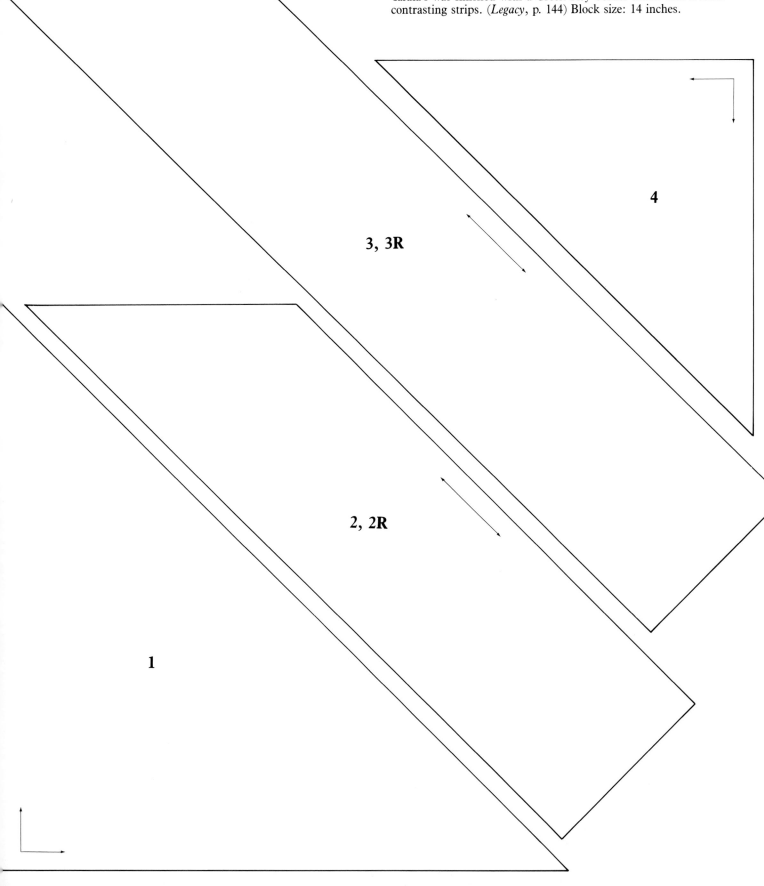

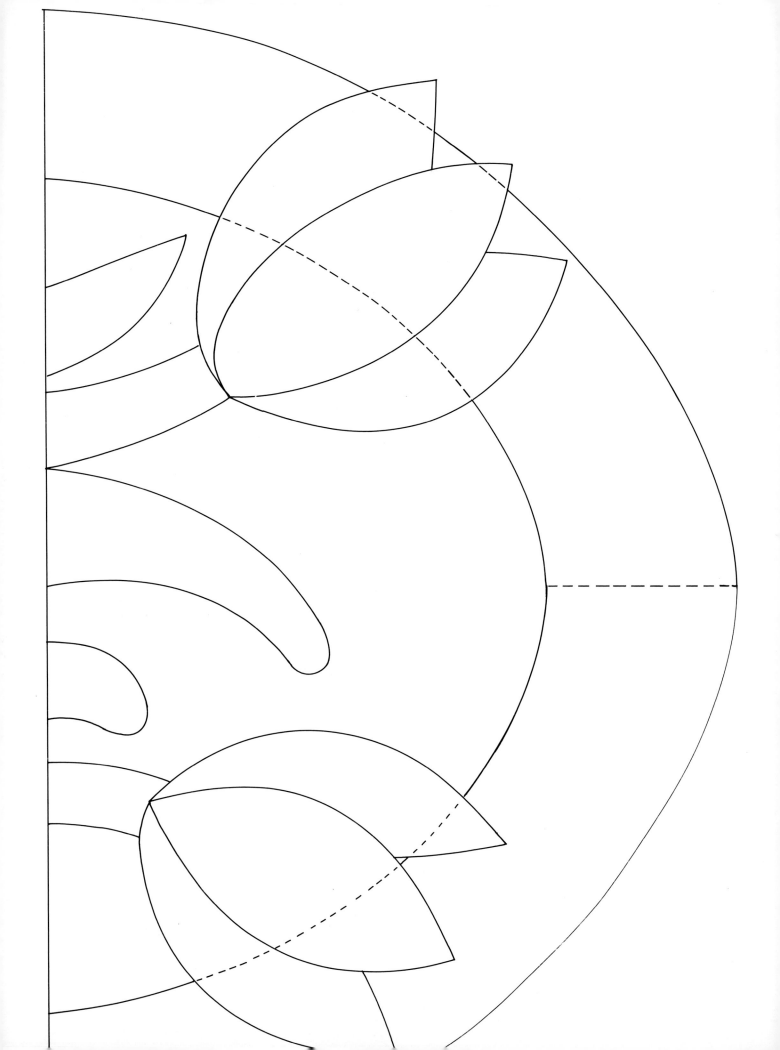

DUTCH TULIP (1990)   Michelle Fitch

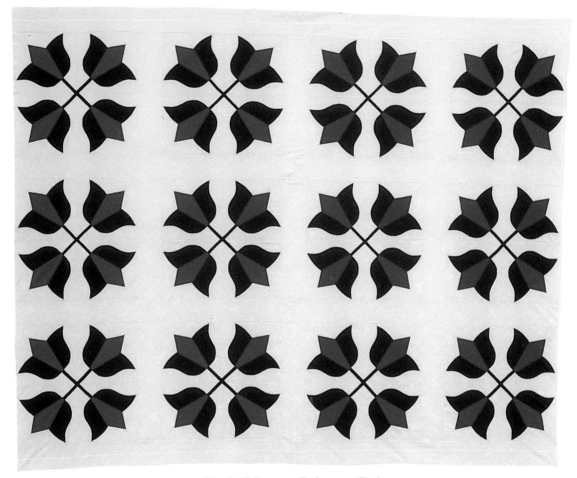

Dutch Tulip, *unquilted top*   *(Fitch)*

TALULA BOTTOMS' aunt, Jerusha Murphy Rogers, was her mother's sister and the fifth member of her close family to die, directly or indirectly, as a result of the Civil War in Georgia. In the 1850s she made the old quilt from which this pattern was drafted. Jerusha's son, Charles, grew up in the Gilbert household after both of his parents died in the 1870s. He may have given his mother's quilt to Talula, who was not to inherit one of her own mother's quilts (*Legacy*, 81, 84).

For a long time, until many fragments of information were put together, mystery accompanied this old quilt. The note attached to the quilt by Talula's daughter Almira some years after Talula's death attributed it to "Jerusha Gilbert, Almira's grandmother." Knowing Almira's maternal grandmother was not Jerusha but Holly Murphy Gilbert, I began a search for Murphy family records and found that Murphys had lived in the Carolinas and Georgia and that some had become Mormons and moved to Utah. Eventually I was led to the name Jerutia Demaris Murphy, younger sister of Holly Duke Murphy (Gilbert), in a journal that their father, John Mark Murphy, had kept from 1830 until his death in 1862.[5] (Other sources spell her name Jerusha.) The most complete history of the descendants of John Mark Murphy was obtained from Salt Lake City records. My curiosity about the *Dutch Tulip* quilt gave me an unexpected bonus in learning some-thing of the history of my maternal great-grandmother Gilbert's family.

Jerusha's quilt is water-stained and fragile, though exquisitely pieced and quilted. It is pieced with one-eighth-inch seams, easily eye-measured, a practice that requires no marking of seams and effects perfect corners and accurate easing of curved shapes. An identically pieced *Tulip*, made in the same Prussian blue color but set together with matching pieced sashing, may have been made by Talula's mother, Holly Murphy Gilbert. It was found with Holly's great-great-grandson in Fayette County, Georgia, in 1989. Its edges were never bound. The history contained in this worn and water-stained 1850s or 1860s quilt was swept away by the Civil War and its aftermath in Georgia. In 1864, with General Sherman poised to move on his cruel promise "to make Georgia howl," Holly's family fled Fayette County for safety. It was November, and in covered wagon travel, quilts were needed for warmth and comfort for the four children, devoted blacks, and a pregnant mother. For Holly's family—and her quilts—life was forever disrupted.

There are innumerable tulip quilt designs, most of them appliqué patterns. I have called both Jerusha's and the Gilbert quilt *Dutch Tulip*, from a similar pieced pattern in *Hope Winslow's Quilt Book* found in Talula's pattern collection.[6] The *Dutch Tulip* was a popular pattern during the 1850s, according to Mary Elizabeth Johnson.[7]

Dutch Tulip *Detail (c. 1855) Jerusha Murphy Rogers*

Gilbert Family Quilt (c. 1855) (Photo Courtesy John Lynch)

The large pieces in this pieced tulip block (only the stem is appliquéd) make it easy to piece, despite the curved patches. Four tulips make a 17½-inch block. Block size: 17½-inches.

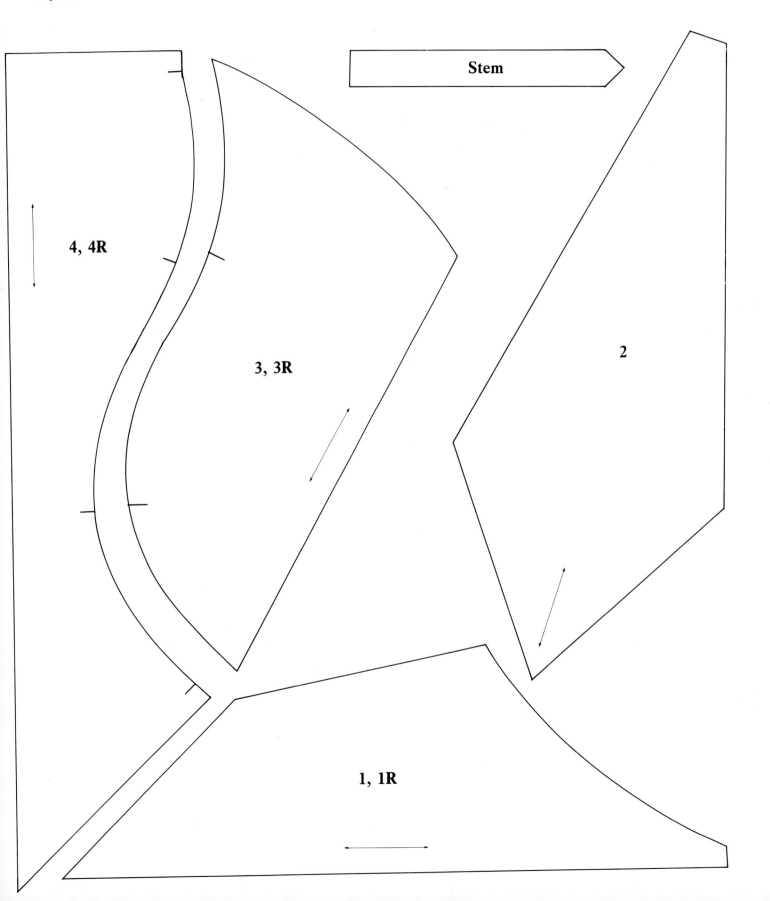

Stem

4, 4R

3, 3R

2

1, 1R

FANCY DRESDEN PLATE (1990) Michelle Fitch

Fancy Dresden Plate   *(Fitch)*

FIVE OF TALULA'S quilts in this popular 1930s design, identical except for the cotton prints that vary from quilt to quilt, have been well-preserved. Another well-worn one survives, and saved letters suggest Talula may have made others on order.[8] All utilize for accent the same red-and-yellow Ely and Walker calico found in several of Talula's quilts dating from 1890 through 1940. She kept a bolt of this and a matching green calico always handy in her quilt closet, and she often used the two colors together for pieced sashing (*Legacy*, 153).

One *Dresden Plate* quilt was bestowed on her foster son Carl Leake as a reward for his heroic actions, when at the risk of his own life he saved a man trapped in a cotton gin fire. (Later Carl's own house burned, but the quilt was merely scorched because it was stored with other quilts in a metal trunk.) Another, a gift from Talula to her sister Nannie Dickson's daughter, was recently found in a trunk in Fayetteville, Georgia, along with eight other quilts, most of them preserved like new.

The design appeared in the 1930s in *Successful Farming*, a magazine to which the family subscribed. The pattern illustrated here was drafted directly from one of Talula's quilts.

Fancy Dresden Plate *Detail   (c. 1935)   Talula Gilbert Bottoms*

The extended reel "arms" across the surface of the plate result in an interesting consistency for a scrap quilt or, as in Michelle's example, afford a striking use of contemporary fabrics. The "plate" is first pieced, then appliquéd onto a background block. Block size: 14 inches.

4

1

2

3

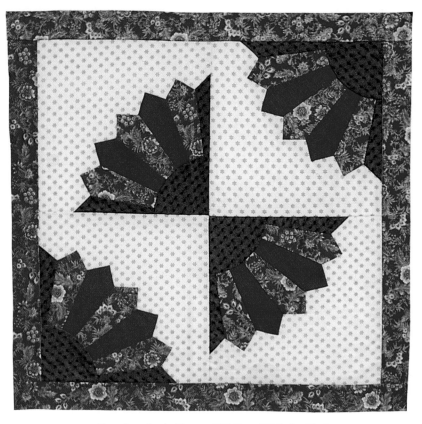

Grandmother's Fan   *(1990)*   *Michelle Fitch*

TALULA'S MUCH USED and faded fan quilt was found with her grandson's family in April 1990 in Michigan. Talula had given it to her son Roger, perhaps as a wedding present, soon after it was made. Only one of that family's quilts, a 1928 *Lone Star* that had come to Roger's daughter-in-law through Talula's daughter Mollie Ruth, had been found until the *Fan* quilt appeared. Its discovery then led to others: a very old *Wandering Foot*, a 1930s *Fancy Dresden Plate*, and a quilt made in pink and white by a 1932 pattern called *Around the Chimney*.[9]

The poignant and rich story of Roger's efforts to move beyond his humble beginnings, to educate himself and fulfill his destiny as an inventive chemist, is only hinted at in *Legacy* (135–136). It is recorded further in letters to his parents, in Almira's genealogy, and in numerous scientific journals and books.[10] But the tangible evidence of the undying love of a mother for a son whose twentieth-century genius created a distance beyond her comprehension, remains today in the quilts she made and gave to him.

The fan pattern included here was drafted from Talula's quilt. Michelle's example, in process, will be a special Christmas piece.

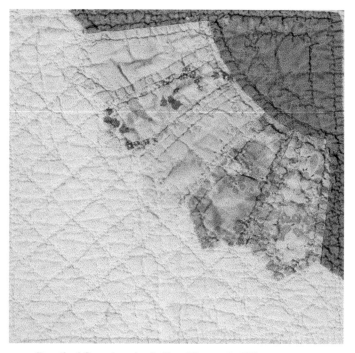

Detail of Grandmother's Fan *(Bottoms). (Photo courtesy Dafydd Bottoms)*

The "fan" is pieced and then appliquéd onto an 11-inch background square. By departing from the traditional setting of the fan blocks in one direction, Michelle and Talula increased the appearance of swinging motion in the quilt. Block size: 10½ inches.

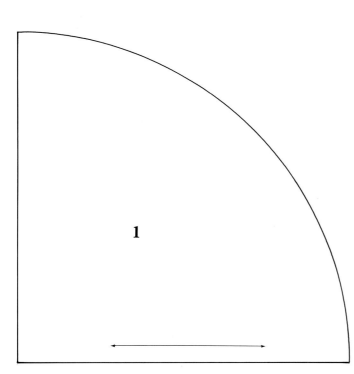

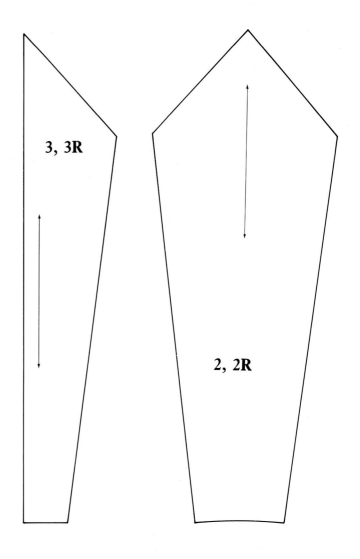

PINEY (PEONY) (1990) Dorothy Frost

Lavender Piney *(c. 1935) Talula Gilbert Bottoms*

TALULA MADE two *Piney* quilts from the same pattern, one pink and one lavender. Both are more complex than the one described in Carlie Sexton's booklet, *Yesterday's Quilts in Homes of Today*[11] (*Legacy*, 143). The flower in the Sexton quilt is made of one piece, whereas Talula's has ten pieced petals and her design has four rather than two leaves. She gave the lavender quilt top, with its unusual border of shirred "piney" buds, to her foster son Carl Leake's wife Merle. It was later to be inherited by their youngest daughter, who has recently had it quilted. Carl and Merle lived nearby with their four daughters, the only one of Talula and Tom Bottoms' "descendants" to remain their neighbors close enough to be on call in emergencies.

No pattern source has been found for Talula's quilts; as with a number of others, this pattern was drafted directly from Talula's *Piney.*

Dorothy's wall hanging combines four flowers into a one-blocked appliqué design, whereas in Talula's quilt the design is created by four blocks, with a small appliqué quatrefoil covering the intersection of the stems.

Piney *(Frost)*

To create the effect of a rotating pattern, a 24-inch block with four flowers, first piece your "pineys" with ten petals each. Cut four 12-inch squares of background fabric (12½″ with seams added) and appliqué stems and leaves (two from right-hand corners, two from left), then appliqué the flowers over the ends of stems. Stitch the four squares together, stems at center, and finally appliqué the quarterfoil piece at the intersection point in the center of the 24-inch block. Block size: 12 inches.

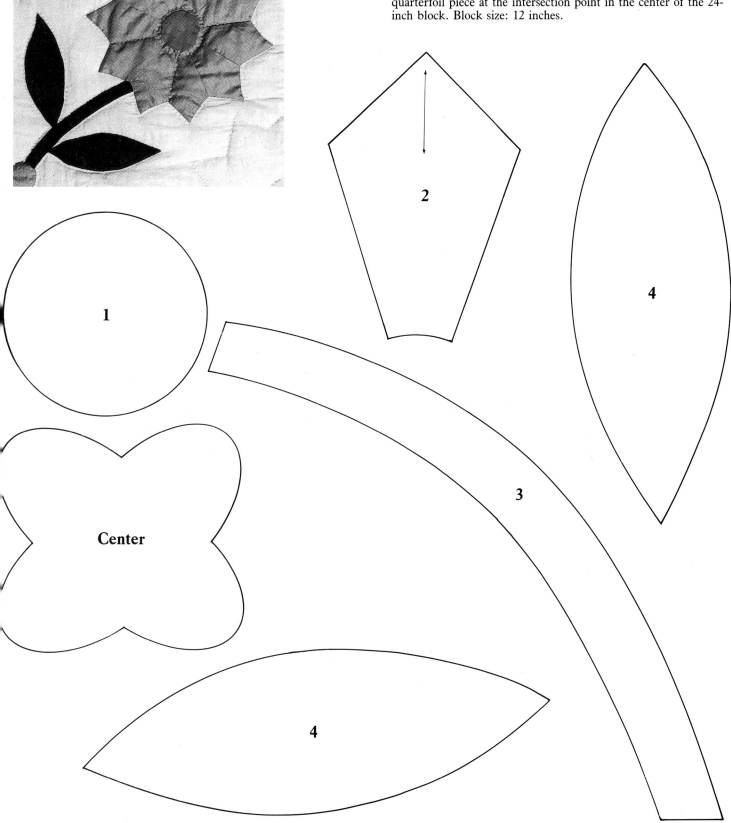

PEAR BASKET (1989-1990) Pieced by Nancilu Burdick★

Detail of Pear Basket *(c. 1860)* *Elisa McElroy Bottoms*

AS TALULA WROTE her memoir in 1943, she reminisced: "Then as they married, I gave a nice quilt to each. Ary got the Basket of Flowers, Matt got Basket of Pears, Emmett got Magnolia Leaf, Roger got The Road to Texas, I think. . . ."

With six living sons and only two daughters (who gave up quilting as young women), Talula happily continued the old custom of providing the necessary utility quilts and at least one special quilt for her children. Most of them simply took the quilts for granted; they were cover, in sickness and in health, for their growing families. Even some of the "nice" quilts were used every day and worn out, often from necessity. It was customary for the older children to take a favorite quilt to college, and later *their* children used them in vans and station wagons, on picnics and family vacations. Such was the story of the *Pear Basket* as well as innumerable other quilts.

Talula may have drafted her *Pear Basket* pattern from memory, from the one made by her mother-in-law Elisa and given to an older son, who had moved away. The odd raised pedestal and un-even rectangular pieces give the quilt a primitive quality unlike other family *Pear Basket* quilts. Talula gave hers to her son Matt at his marriage in 1914, and it came down through the years, after hard use and much travel, to Talula's great-grandson in Texas (*Legacy*, 123).

Talula's sister Nannie's *Pear Basket*, found in Georgia in 1989, was preserved in like-new condition. Both Talula's and Nannie's quilts, as well as Elisa's, demonstrate the artistry of stylized design practiced by nineteenth-century country women; the unevenness in Nannie's drooping fruit only adds to its charm. Both Talula's and Nannie's patterns, Talula's slightly adjusted for ease in piecing, were drafted from the original quilts.

Pear Basket *(Burdick)*

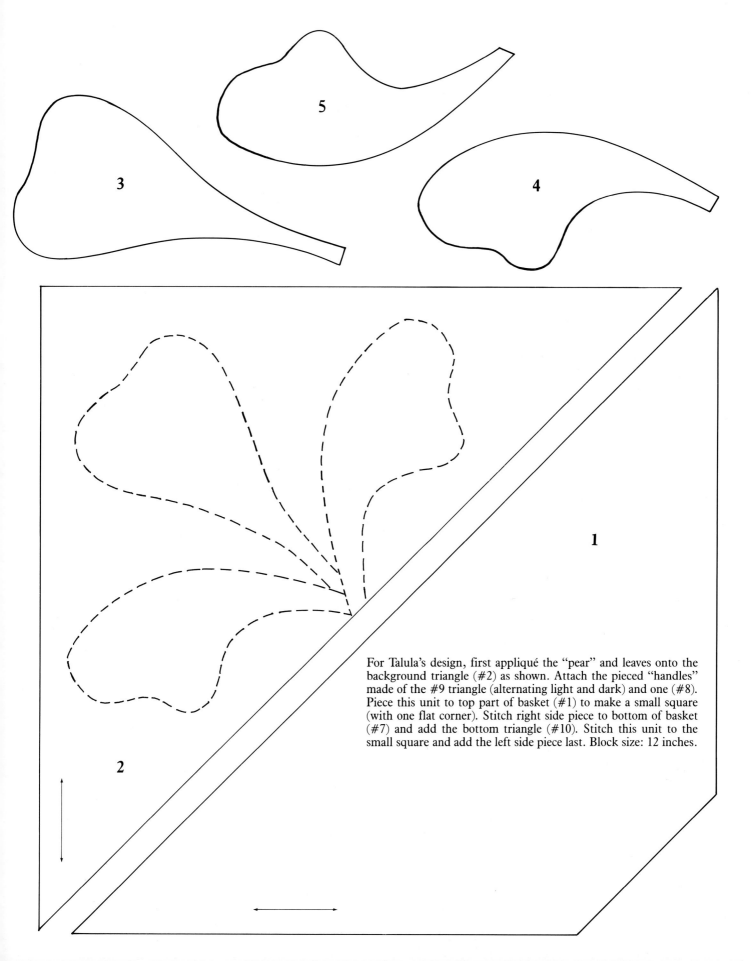

For Talula's design, first appliqué the "pear" and leaves onto the background triangle (#2) as shown. Attach the pieced "handles" made of the #9 triangle (alternating light and dark) and one (#8). Piece this unit to top part of basket (#1) to make a small square (with one flat corner). Stitch right side piece to bottom of basket (#7) and add the bottom triangle (#10). Stitch this unit to the small square and add the left side piece last. Block size: 12 inches.

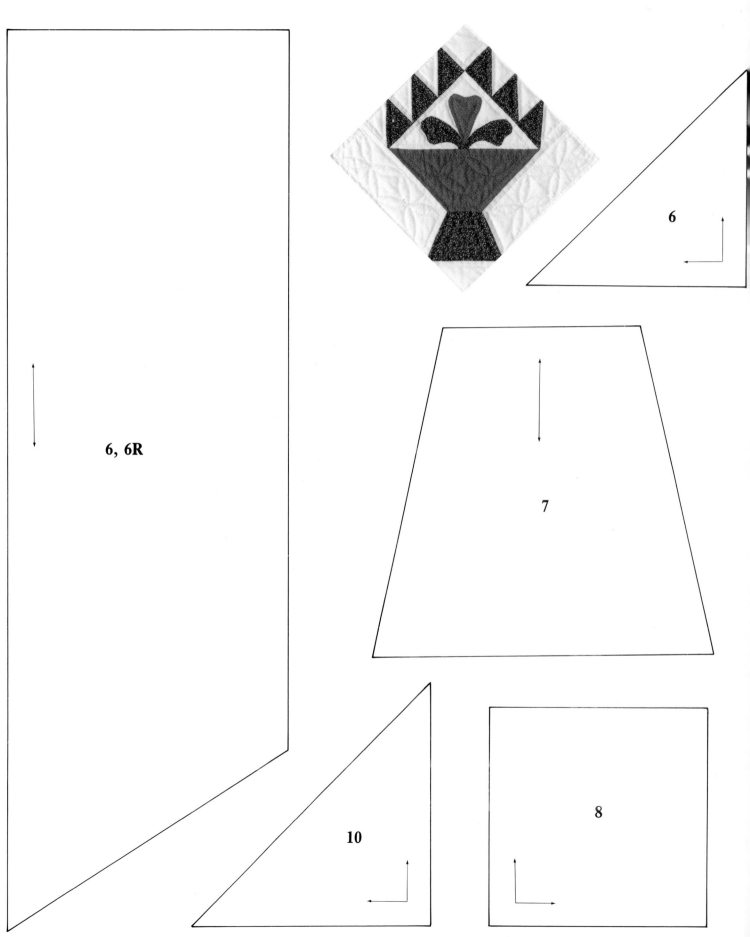

6, 6R

6

7

10

8

Nannie's design is made of two triangles, one pieced (the basket) and one appliquéd. Piece light and dark triangles (#4) and join to the base (#2) with right side piece and lower triangle (#1) already attached. Add left side piece, as in Talula's block, to complete the square. Block size: 12 inches.

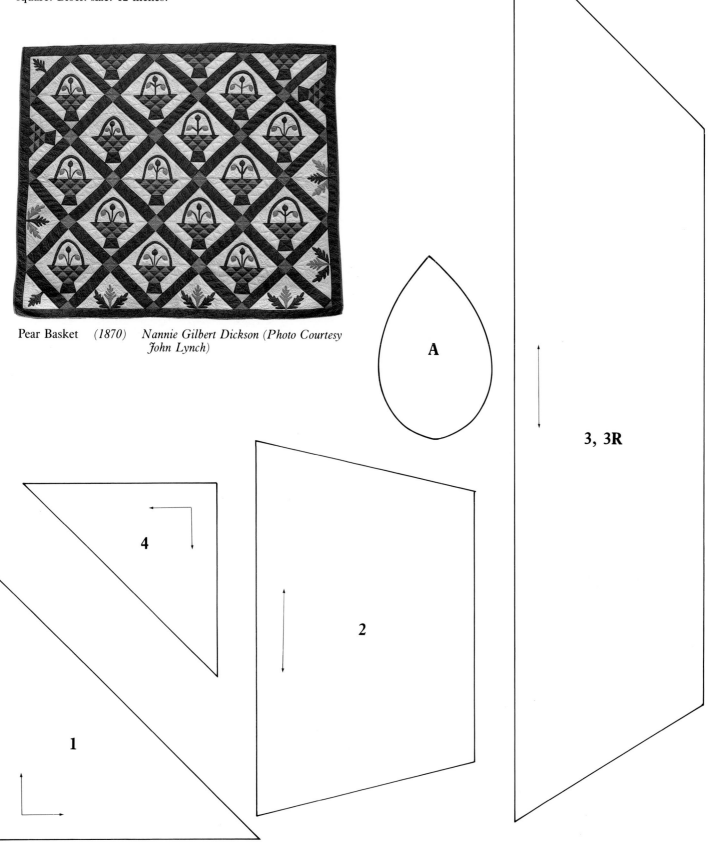

Pear Basket   (1870)   Nannie Gilbert Dickson (Photo Courtesy John Lynch)

A

3, 3R

4

2

1

ORANGE BUD (1989) Michelle Fitch

Orange Bud   *(Fitch)*

IN MAKING HER *Orange Bud* wall piece, Michelle challenged herself to create the effect of age and distinction resembling the work of superb nineteenth-century quilters. (Her quilting design is from a blown-up photograph of Mary Elizabeth Harris' 1865 quilt (*Legacy*, 81). Michelle proved to all of us that this seemingly difficult pattern can be pieced with ease and with a fine sense of achievement. Her experience demonstrates how we so often limit ourselves by our own narrow conception of what our hands can do.

The *Orange Bud* made by Talula in the late 1800s has not been found, nor has her mother Holly Gilbert's mid-1800s quilt of the same design. Nonetheless, those quilts have been a central motivating factor in my work as a quiltmaker and writer (*Legacy*, 10). In addition, the quilt like Talula's, found in Georgia and pictured in *Legacy*, has fostered a strong bond with my Gilbert cousins in Fayette County and has enabled me to make a vital connection with my maternal roots. Such synchronicity is often the result of a serious search for the artifact that contains a truth one is seeking.[12] Many quilt historians have found this to be the case; the object or information sought may not be found, but an opening to greater surprises and a more significant life experience result from the endeavor.

While I searched, the urge to make an *Orange Bud* quilt grew more intense, but inexperienced as I was, my attempt to draft a true pieced pattern proved futile. Nonetheless, my desire prompted me to appliqué the quilt illustrated here. The pieced one will come later, for I continue to learn (by Michelle's example) that patience and persistence are important components in achievement and in the realization of one's untapped capacities.

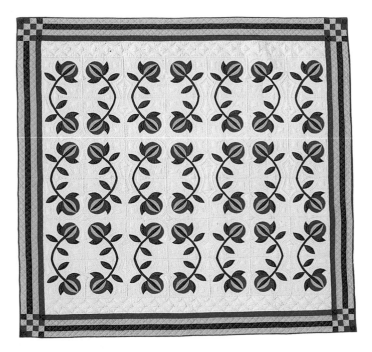

Orange Bud   *(1986)   Appliquéd by Nancilu Burdick★*

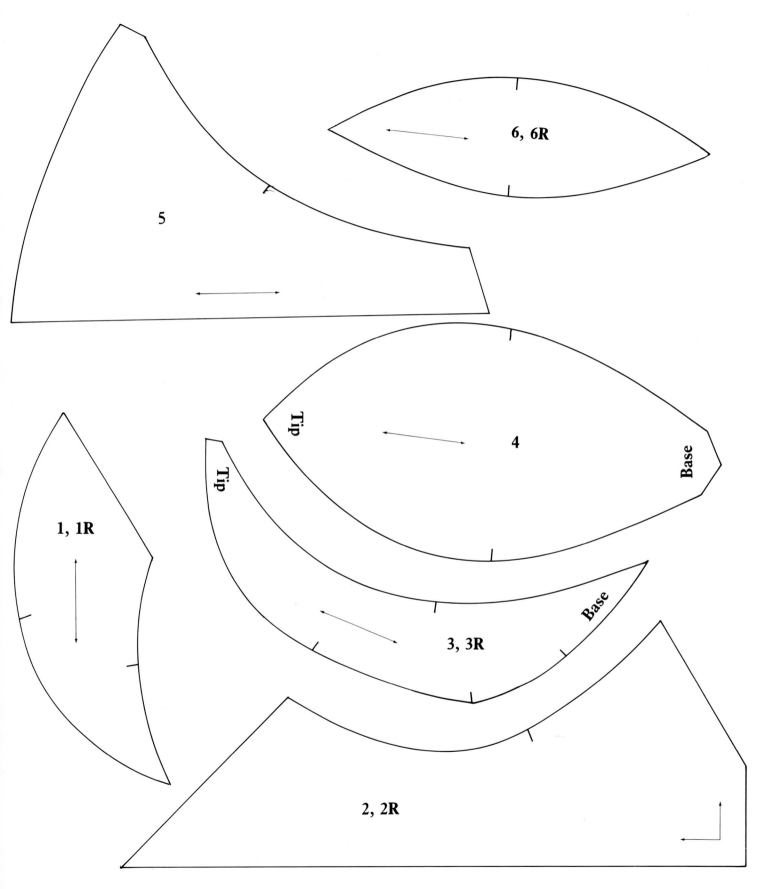

5

6, 6R

Tip

Base

4

1, 1R

Tip

Base

3, 3R

2, 2R

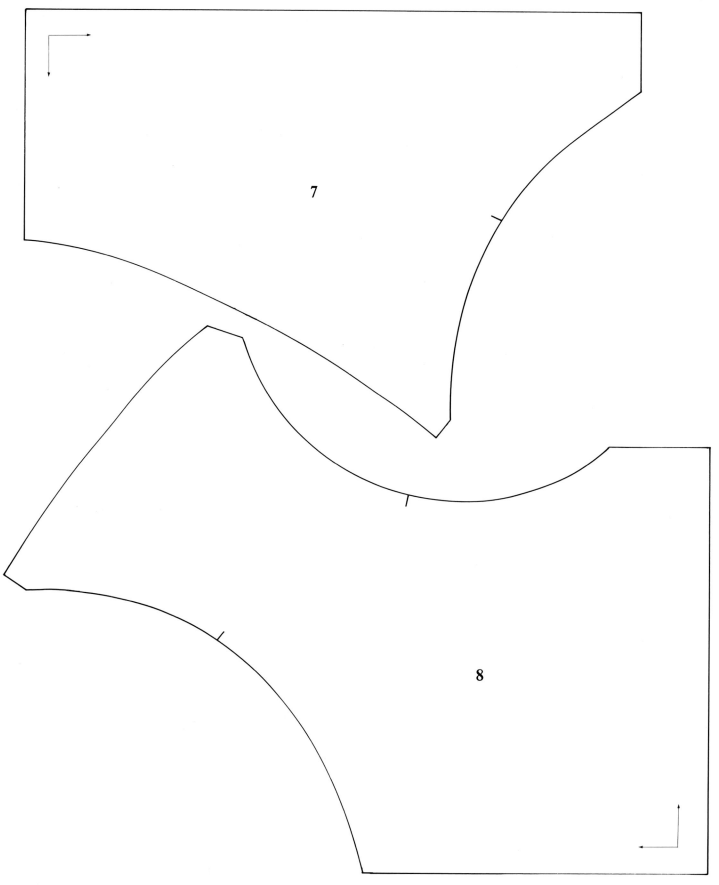

This complex design is highly rewarding to hand piece, though it can be easily appliquéd. To piece the block, precision is essential and begins with cutting. Pieces 1, 2, and 3; pieces 1, 2, and 3R may be cut together *with good scissors* by folding fabric, right sides together, eight or more layers at a time. Michelle pieced these together with the calix leaves (7 and 7R), then added on the corner pieces above the "bud." After piecing right and left sides of the lower portion, she joined them at center and carefully pin-basted this section to the flower before handstitching the block together. The stem is appliquéd to cover the seam and extends just to the upper corner of the bud. Patience and hand-sewing are recommended to achieve a perfectly square block. Block size: 11 inches.

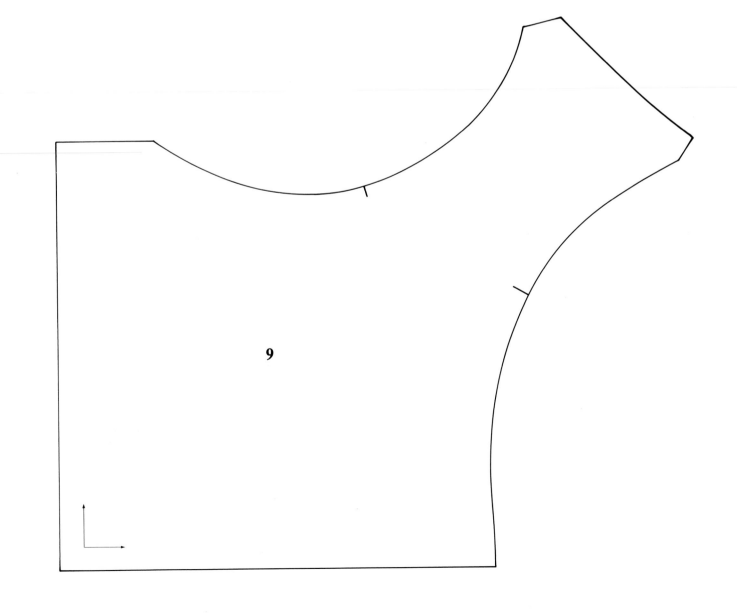

9

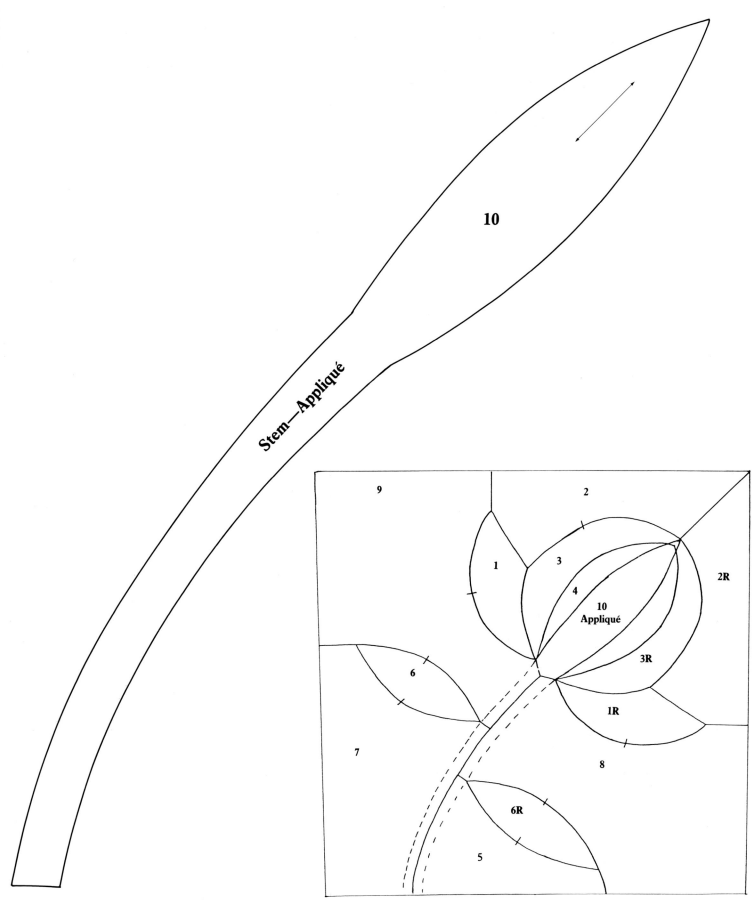

Stem—Appliqué

10

PART III

APPLIQUÉ QUILTS

Feather III   (1989–1990)   *Frances Vining*

APPLIQUÉ QUILTS

Appliqué lends itself to such elaborate, elegant, and creative of designs as one finds in Baltimore Album quilts; yet in some ways it can be the simplest. Giving full reign to the imagination, one can use shapes, patterns, or pictures of one's choice on blocks or on the full quilt without thought of following someone else's design precisely. Freedom of expression, improvisation, and symbolic representation of ideas and feelings all become available in appliqué even to novice quilters.

As can be seen on the walls of thousands of church school rooms everywhere, appliqué is an ideal medium for children, as well as for the most sophisticated adult quilter and artist. Moreover, many gifted, self-taught quiltmakers, untrained as artists, are being recognized today for their unique, often called primitive, appliqué work, some of it eagerly sought by folk art museums and collectors. Yet fine appliqué work requires aesthetic sense, steady hands, and good eyesight. Talula began early to do "laid work" as she called it, developed a high degree of skill, and continued even with complex flower patterns, until she was almost eighty (*Legacy*, 144). Of Talula's approximately 130 quilts remaining today almost one-third are wholly or partially appliquéd.

The appliqué patterns presented here are not intricate, and most are simple enough for a beginning quilter. Used skillfully, they lend themselves to innovation and can be made into impressive quilts.

Detail of Garden Bouquet *(c. 1935)* *Talula Bottoms*

BUTTERFLY (c. 1930) Talula Bottoms

Butterfly   *(Bottoms)*

AMONG CARRIE A. HALL'S collection of quilt patches is a geometric pieced butterfly she called "a favorite old-time pattern." Whatever the origin, butterflies were a favorite design among country women throughout the South after 1930, though most were appliquéd. Such quilts in bright and often gaudy colors are still frequently seen for sale along roadways, hung on porches or fences to attract passers-by.[1]

Talula made one *Butterfly* quilt that after many years found its way to Nevada, where it was discovered in 1985. She made it in such subdued colors it seems not to belong to the pastels and gay prints so characteristic of the Great Depression era. Each approximately eight-inch butterfly utilizes a different figured or plaid cotton for the wings, the patterns appliquéd by embroidery in the simplest of stitches—Talula called the decorative running stitch she used "saddle stitch"—on an eleven-inch unbleached muslin background. Solid color bodies accent the various prints in the wings, and the whole is unified by the soft yellows of the sashing and the setting squares.

The pattern here was drafted directly from Talula's quilt. Michelle has used bright, hand-dyed colors to reflect off each other, in direct contrast to Talula's quilt on which the colors blend together.

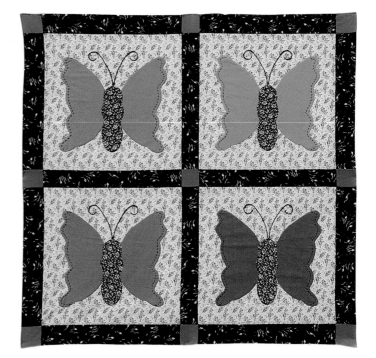

Butterfly   *(1990)   Michelle Fitch*

Talula basted under ⅛-inch edges of the wings, then used black embroidery thread to "saddle-stitch" them to the 12-inch muslin squares. She applied the solid-color bodies between the wings in the same manner before completing the butterfly with French-knot eyes and outline-stitched antennae. Michelle blind-stitched on the wings and body before decorating her block with embroidery. Block size: 11 inches.

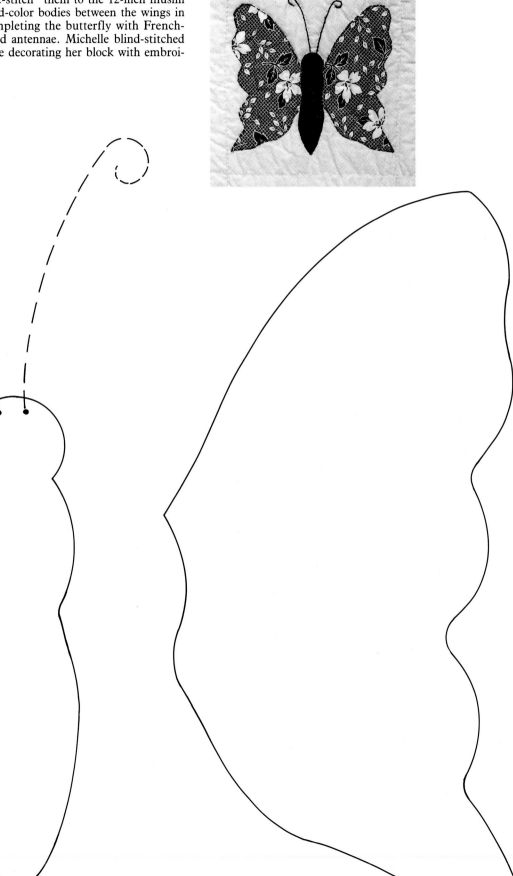

DUTCH DOLL (1989) Michelle Fitch

TALULA BEGAN making her series of "little girl" quilts in the late 1920s at the request of a granddaughter only five or six years old. Lula, named for her grandmother, was about to move to a distant state. Of course Talula could not refuse her, though she had twelve other granddaughters (and two more would come along later). Talula then proceeded to make quilts for all her granddaughters, at least six of them by this pattern, varying the setting design, the colors, and the numbers of "dolls." Talula used an assortment of prints for the dresses, matching solid colors for hats and sleeves, and black for the shoes and the feather stitching on hats and dresses. Her "dolls" walk up and down or around the quilts as if they represent her own innumerable steps as a mother, queen of her household.

On one *Dutch Doll*, made for the daughter of her oldest son, instead of making French Knots down the front, Talula sewed on the saved buttons from her son's baby dresses. How dearly that well-worn quilt is still treasured by Talula's great-granddaughter.

Unlike most of the extremely popular and various *Sunbonnet Sue* quilts made in great numbers (*ad nauseum*, some would say) during the twenties and thirties, Talula's girls, with their ample bosoms, look more like proud little women (*Legacy*, 131).

Reflecting contemporary concerns for the environment, Michelle has "recycled" old fabrics in her *Dutch Doll* wall hanging. The only new material is in the border.

Dutch Doll

Talula turned under the ⅛-inch edges of each piece, probably without basting, and blind-stitched them to the center of a 10-inch muslin square prior to embroidering with feather stitching and French knots in black. (See page 72 of Bets Ramsey's *Old and New Quilts in the Southern Tradition*.) Block size: 10 inches.

SUNBONNET SUE (1989) Appliquéd and embroidered by Nancilu Burdick★

SUNBONNET SUE patterns abound, as do stories, jests, and charming fantasies about the sometimes maligned little girl hiding her face behind her hat. So why offer one here? Admittedly, in part it is for sentimental reasons. But also it is a simple pattern that appeals to little girls and can be the first appliqué and embroidery experience for a daughter or granddaughter. Some daughters may want to incorporate pieces of their own favorite outgrown dresses. Too, the simplicity of the design appeals to those who want to make a handmade quilt in a short time.

The quilt illustrated here was one of two made for granddaughters, with their help, from a pattern drafted from one of Talula's 1930s quilts (*Legacy*, 131) that was inherited by a great-great granddaughter. Julie Anna was sixteen and thinking of college when the borrowed quilt was returned to her. She hugged it close and buried her face in it in an unforgettable gesture of love for its maker, a "grandmother" she had never known. What better reason to make another *Sunbonnet Sue*? These little bonneted girls, descended from the nineteenth-century author Kate Greenaway's children through the little girls in Bertha Corbett's *The Sunbonnet Babies Primer* (c. 1900), are still appealing and lend themselves to imaginative treatment as well as to the traditional design illustrated here.[2]

Detail of Sunbonnet Sue

Sunbonnet Sue

This simplest of designs can easily be accomplished in your favorite method of appliqué. Talula turned under ⅛-inch seam allowances with a few basting stitches, pinned the design in place, and "saddle stitched" it on an 11½-inch square of muslin. For my quilts, I basted the design on (after basting under ⅛-inch seams), blind stitched it, and then added the embroidery. For the shoes, I used paper templates under the fabric for smoother edges. Block size: 11 inches.

BRING BACK THE BLUEBIRDS   (1990)   Frances B. Vining

THE INSPIRATION for this quilt was Talula's *Bluebirds in Easy Appliqué*. This pattern could be ordered for ten cents in February 1936, from the Women's Service Bureau of the *Nashville Banner* (*Legacy*, 145–146). With prayerful heart, Talula sent for the pattern, cut the templates from brown paper, then made and tied the "bluebirds" comforter for a frail granddaughter threatened with tuberculosis. Even while she was making it, a niece who lived nearby died of the malady. In those days, tuberculosis meant almost certain death. The disease took Talula's mother in 1865 at age thirty-one, and before the end of the century, five more of her close family members. Talula may have chosen black for a number of the birds as a profound symbol or simply to suit her own aesthetic sense. Regardless, Ruth, the granddaughter, believes to this day that the cheerful, warm quilt made from "recycled" old clothes and wool from her father's sheep, with its "bluebirds of happiness" and the grandmother's love it represented, were responsible for her healing. Talula saved the clipping and the brown paper patterns, each charming bird template perforated with pinholes, indicating that she also considered the quilt significant.

Frances's contemporary and cheerful interpretation of Talula's quilt was thoughtfully handmade from natural materials. It reflects an ecological theme, the three-dimensional effect achieved by the attic-window setting suggesting the depth and significance of such concerns today. It is an appropriate reminder of how changed the world is since the 1930s. Talula's quilt was made during the Great Depression from salvaged parts of worn-out clothes that had already been "recycled" as hand-me-downs. It was a time when bluebirds in great numbers were the cheerful "harbingers of spring." Recycling was stark necessity then, unlike today when new cloth is plentiful and bluebirds are almost extinct. Yet many impressive quilts were made then, as now, attesting to women's ingenuity and yearning for beauty in the face of Spartan conditions.[3]

Bring Back the Bluebirds

Clipping ordered from the Nashville Banner (*1936*)

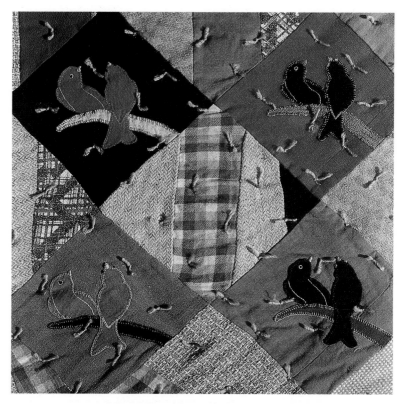

Detail of Talula's Bluebirds   *(c. 1936)*

Talula at the well on the farm near Athens, Alabama (1938)

This appealing design hardly needs comment; its name indicates the ease with which it can be accomplished. Fran has created an interesting contemporary piece in her setting, with a minimum of embroidery. Talula applied her design (without turning under edges) with a few basting stitches. She finished the edges with buttonhole stitching and detailed the wings and eyes in simple "rope" or outline and the tail with chain stitching. Block size: 8¾ inches.

TALULA'S TULIP (1990) Dorothy Frost

Talula's Tulip   *(Frost)*

THIS PATTERN is called *Talula's Tulip* simply because it was drafted directly from her late 1930s *Tulip* quilt and because no other pattern source has been found. It was one of the last "laid work" quilts she made, for by age eighty-one she had become "too nervous" to do the careful work she demanded of herself and her eyes tired more easily when she tried to do the close work required for appliqué (*Legacy*, 159). The quilt top was left to her son Burrell and his wife Alice, who quilted it in the 1940s. It was later inherited by their daughter Mary, for whom Talula had earlier made two special quilts, the *Princess Feather* and one of her *Dutch Doll* quilts (*Legacy*, 129, 142). Mary was the only child of Tom and Talula's son Burrell, to whom they had deeded the "home place." Mary was the joy of her grandmother's old age; she inherited eighteen of Talula's quilts. "Burlie" raise cotton and developed a prize dairy herd and one of the finest orchards in North Alabama. Many letters from Talula to her are filled with stories of "Mary picking cotton," "Mary's little lamb," or "Mary bringing in wood for our fire." She was the only one of Talula's twenty-five grandchildren with whom she had daily contact until the end of her life.

Mary and her prize cow

Dorothy, who is a quilting teacher, uses an "old-fashioned" appliqué method; she bastes under the edges of each piece, 3/16- or 1/4-inch all around. Then she bastes the whole design in place before blind-stitching it to complete the block. The use of bold colors is characteristic of much of Dorothy's work. Block size: 8¾ inches by 10 inches.

MAGNOLIA LEAF (1990) Frances B. Vining

Magnolia Leaf   *(Vining)*

TWO IDENTICAL nineteenth-century quilts in this design remain in like-new condition today, one made by Talula (c. 1880), and one by her sister, Nannie Gilbert Dickson (c. 1870) (*Legacy*, 72). The heart designs in the quilting of both suggest that in spite of their burdensome household duties as young girls after the Civil War had so disrupted their lives, the sisters made their own bridal quilts. The quilts have identical oak-leaf borders on just two sides, indicating they were made for best "parlor" beds that were pushed into a corner so that only two edges of the quilt would show.

Nannie's quilt was found by her granddaughter Alice Lynch in 1989 in a trunk in Fayetteville, Georgia, along with seven other quilts left by Nannie's youngest daughter, Johnnie May Dickson Dorman, who died in 1986. The quilts had been stored away so long that no one remembered ever having seen them.

Talula's *Magnolia Leaf* was found in Ohio with a great-granddaughter. Charlotte, who also inherited another of Talula's very early quilts, *The Baby Bunting* (*Legacy*, 69), was astonished to learn the age and significance of the almost perfectly preserved quilt and to know how it must have been treasured by her great-grandmother. When Charlotte entered the *Magnolia Leaf* in the Zoar Valley, Ohio, historical society quilt show in 1987, it won second place in the antique category.

In this contemporary expression of Talula's *Magnolia Leaf*, Frances stresses the delicacy of the magnolia blossom by using creamy pale pink chintz as a background for the leaf motif. The quilting "in-the-ditch" gives a subtle reflecting texture, which suggests the lights and shadows of a southern summer day.

Detail of Magnolia Leaf   *(c. 1870)*
Nannie Gilbert Dickson

Frances pin-basted the pieces on her background material step by step, beginning with the reel (moon) shapes. She turned under the edges with her needle as she blind-stitched them on. She finds this is the simplest and fastest appliqué method for her, although it requires much experience to do it easily. "Each quilter must find the technique that works best for herself," she said. Block size: 16 inches.

IVY BASKET (1990) Frances B. Vining

THE PATTERN for this basket block, based on a quilt Talula is thought to have made and given to her son Emmett, was sketched from descriptions given by two of Talula's grandchildren, using actual ivy leaves on a plain basket. Talula's own quilt may have been quite different, although one of Emmett's children who had seen it remembered it vividly enough to describe the pattern as it is shown here. The Palladian window setting for the basket of ivy was conceived by Frances Vining and designed to reflect the popular window style used in so many contemporary homes. Other quilters may improvise further.

Ivy Basket   (*Vining*)

There is nothing difficult about this basket pattern, although one needs to remember to clip the concave points of the leaves before basting (or pinbasting) them on. It is also a good idea to trace first with pencil on the background square the particular positions of the stems and leaves. The final step for Frances was embroidering the stems. Block size: 12 inches.

FEATHER (1990) Interpretations by Frances B. Vining

After the children began to appear [there was one each year for 5 or 6 years] the nice pretty tops had to lay away in a trunk until I could have a little time to quilt them. . . . When I quilted the Feather quilt I had [a baby in the cradle] and 3 little boys . . . and they liked to play in the yard. But it was funny to them for one at a time to come in and stand by me while I quilted and fan me with a large palmetto fan. When one was tired I had him go out and let another come in to fan me. Now this is the history of the Feather quilt.[4]

IN TALULA'S *FEATHER,* appliquéd and quilted in the old Fayette County, Georgia, log home where her husband Tom was born, the heart-shaped arrangement of plumes in pairs facing each other, creates feminine, womblike images. With the pattern emphasized by the close echo quilting, the overall effect is one of rhythmic movement. In a letter to her daughter Mollie Ruth in December 1940, Talula reveals a joyous intensity in telling her "the history of the Feather quilt" (*Legacy,* 90, 92). It is as if she had, as Kristen Langellier says, given birth to a truer self in "giving birth" to that special quilt.

Talula had been married for nine years; after three years childless she had borne six children in less than seven years and had lost two of them to "cholera infantum." During that time she had made and quilted many everyday quilts. In 1892, with her first daughter in the cradle, she had decided she could no longer "wait for a little time to quilt the many nice pretty tops" she had also made and laid away in her trunk. She would have to *make* the time. She chose the *Feather* on which to try her skills of nice quilting, and she did it alone, for her

beloved mother-in-law, who had helped her quilt so many others, had died in the flu epidemic of 1891. Completing the *Feather* was a victory Talula still vividly recalled nearly fifty years later.

Frances Vining, who conceived these pieces as a series, was inspired by the flowing feminine motion in Talula's quilt and by the possibilities for contemporary designs based on its pattern. Two sizes of the *Feather* are given here. Frances preferred the reduced design for her series. The larger size can be used to make a full quilt of nine blocks with a truly old-fashioned look.

There was a period when sewing machines were so new that it was not only acceptable but quite fashionable and a mark of status to bind even the best "company" quilts by machine. Often thread different in color from the fabric was used, to deliberately show the machine stitching. In a nineteenth-century quilt it is not uncommon to find machine stitching randomly run across a meticulously hand-appliquéd block or two. At least one such quilt is in the Smithsonian Institution collection. Some women with boldness and skill in manipulating fabric under the presser foot appliquéd beautiful old patterns such as the *Orange Blossom* entirely by machine. Some quilts were even machine quilted in the years before 1900.[5]

Several of Talula's nineteenth-century quilts, including the *Feather,* made entirely by hand except for the deliberate top stitching of the binding, indicate that she, too, was proud to show off the work of her new sewing machine. But with few exceptions she would go on piecing and appliquéing her quilt blocks by hand as long as she lived.

Feather I   *(Vining)*

Detail of Feather   *(1880)   Laura Ann Collins Bottoms*

Frances used the same appliqué method here as she did in the two previous examples. It is important to crease the background block from corner to corner, pressing with an iron, in order to position the plumes accurately. The creases in Talula's quilt can still be seen faintly after more than one hundred years. Block size: 21 inches.

Feather II   *(Vining)*

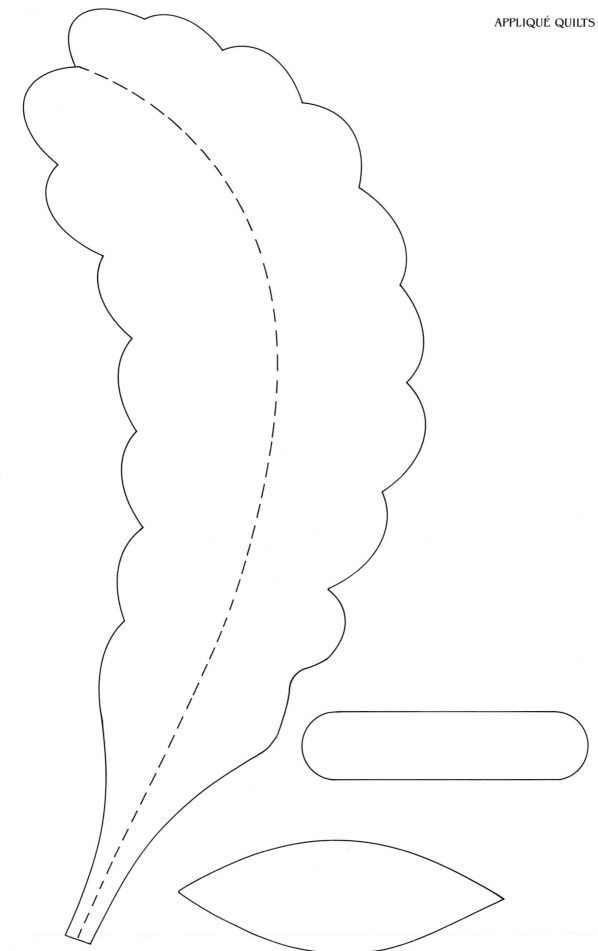

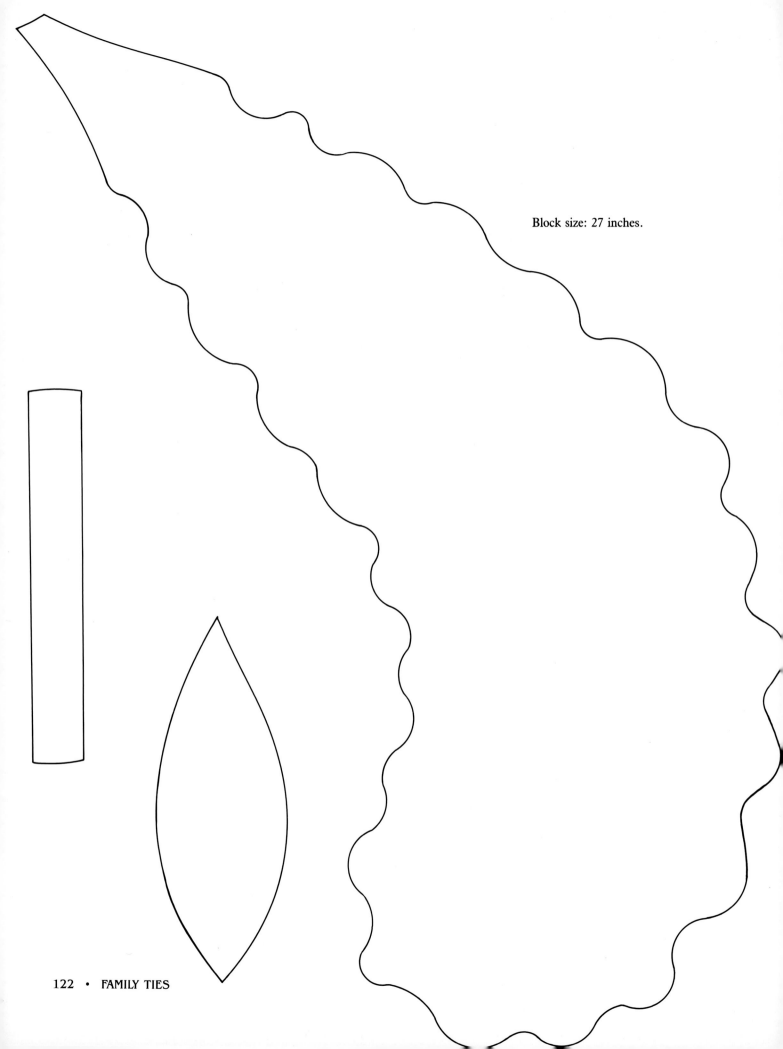

Block size: 27 inches.

NOTES

Introduction

1. Nancilu B. Burdick, *Legacy: The Story of Talula Gilbert Bottoms and Her Quilts* (Nashville: Rutledge Hill Press, 1988).

2. John Naisbitt, *Megatrends* (New York: Warner, 1984), 45.

Continuing the Tradition

1. Delores A. Hinson, *Quilting Manual* (New York: Dover, 1980), 176.

2. Nancy Hoyler, interview with author, Colden, NY, July 1988.

3. Harold Cohen, Ph.D., lecture introducing TAAP, an architecture course for volunteers, State University of New York, Buffalo, 21 Sept. 1983.

4. Alex Haley, *Roots* (New York: Doubleday, 1976).

5. Richard Heinberg, "Looking Back from the End of Time, *Integrity*, (100 Mile House, BC, Integrity International. Jan.–Feb. 1987), 4.

6. Charles Olson, *A Special View of History*, ed. Ann Charters (Berkeley: OYEZ, 1970), 12. In this little-known but significant work, Olson (of the Black Mountain School of Poetry) explains history as the *function* of any one of us; it is what we *do*. See also pp. 25–26.

7. Jeffery Scheuer, "An Interview with Allan Gurganus," *Poets and Writers*, Nov.–Dec. 1990, 25.

8. Florence Y. Wilson, "Why Thanksgiving Day Is Perennial," *Quilter's Newsletter*, Nov. 1972, 7.

9. William Rush Dunton, Jr., M.D., *Old Quilts* (Catonsville, MD: Self-published, 1946), 3–4.

10. Mary Caroline Richards, *Centering in Pottery, Poetry, and the Person* (Middletown, CT: Wesleyan University Press, 1964), 61.

11. Kristin M. Langellier, "Contemporary Quiltmaking Culture in Maine: Tradition and Transition," a paper presented at American Quilt Study Group Symposium, San Rafael, CA, Oct. 1990, scheduled for 1991 publication in that organization's yearbook, *Uncoverings 1990*.

12. Patsy and Myron Orlofsky, *Quilts in America* (New York: McGraw-Hill, 1974), 71.

13. *Ibid.*, 31.

14. Dianne Miller, "Machine Piecing," *Quilter's Newsletter*, July–Aug. 1989, 43.

15. Pat Ferraro, Elaine Hedges, and Julie Silber, *Hearts and Hands: The Influence of Woman and Quilts on American Society* (San Francisco, The Quilt Digest Press), 91.

16. Suellen Myer, "Early Influences of the Sewing Machine and Visible Machine Stitching on Nineteenth-Century Quilts," in *Uncoverings 1989*, ed. Laurel Horton (San Francisco: American Quilt Study Group, 1990), 50–51.

17. Michelle Fitch, interview with author, 28 Aug. 1990.

Part I: Pieced Quilts

1. James Hillman, *Healing Fiction* (Barrytown, NY: Station Hill, 1983), unpaged.

2. Mollie Ruth Bottoms, Journal, 13 July 1939.

3. Letter, Mollie Ruth Bottoms to Ruth B. Potts, Oct. 1974.

4. M. R. Bottoms, Journal, 1939.

5. A later and simpler design was offered in 1936 by Old Chelsea Station, New York, NY. Barbara Brackman, *Encyclopedia of Pieced Quilt Patterns* (Lawrence, KS: Prairie Flower Publishing, 1979 & 1984), no. 1450, 170.

6. Grace Butler Rabatin, interview with author, 17 Apr. 1986.

7. Bertha Clark, interview with author, 13 Apr. 1986. Bertha explained entries in Almira's household ledger 1938–1942, which record payment for sixteen quilts (fourteen by Ruth Martin) and six mattress pads during that period.

8. Carrie A. Hall and Rose G. Kretsinger, *The Romance of the Patchwork Quilt in America* (Caldwell, ID: Caxton Printers, 1935), 48–49.

9. Jinny Beyer, *The Quilter's Album of Blocks and Borders* (McLean, VA: EPM Publications, 1980), 96.

10. Sallie F. Hill, "Eight Star Designs for Patchwork Quilts," *The Progressive Farmer and Southern Ruralist*, nd. Sallie F. Hill was editor of the farm magazine's Home Department, a title that existed only between 1930 and 1935. *See* Erma Kirkpatrick, "Progressive Farmer Quilt References," in *Uncoverings 1985*, ed. Sally Garoutte (Mill Valley, CA: American Quilt Study Group, 1985), 143.

11. Amy Carroll, ed., *The Pattern Library: Patchwork and Appliqué* (New York: Ballantine, 1981), 32. The setting idea for *Tranquility* was suggested by Audrey and Douglas Wiss, *Folk Quilts and How to Recreate Them* (Pittstown, NJ: Main Street, 1983), 19.

12. See Barbara Brackman, *Clues in the Calico* (McLean, VA: EPM Publications, 1989), 19.

13. Edward Binney III, and Gail Binney-Winslow, *Homage to Amanda: Two Hundred Years of American Quilts* (San Francisco: R. K. Press, 1984), 84–91.

14. Almira Bottoms Butler, scrapbook of clippings, letters, and photographs from the last years of T. J. and Talula Bottoms, compiled in 1948. Courtesy Bettie Butler Pearson.

15. Mary Alice Butler, interview with author, 5 June 1986.

16. Letter, Talula Bottoms to Mollie Ruth Bottoms, 16 Sept. 1940. The pattern may have been shown among those published in the 1930s by W. L. M. Clark, Inc., St. Louis, MO. Several pamphlets of these were among Talula's quilt patterns.

17. Letter, Talula Bottoms to Mollie Ruth Bottoms, 17 May 1941.

18. "Does Her Part," *Limestone County Democrat*, nd. Courtesy Bettie Pearson.

19. An identical *Sunflower* quilt is pictured in Patricia Cooper and Norma Bradley Buferd, *The Quilters: Women and Domestic Art—An Oral History* (New York: Doubleday, 1977), 109.

20. Charles Bottoms and Sarah Bottoms Burnash, interviews with author, summer 1985.

21. A very old pattern called *Pickle Dish* (earliest example 1845), of which the *Double Wedding Ring* is a twentieth-century variation, was shown in *Quilter's Newsletter*, no. 148, 7. See also Robert Bishop, *The Romance of the Double Wedding Ring* (New York: E. P. Dutton, 1989), 26.

22. Nancilu Burdick, "Talula Gilbert Bottoms and Her Quilts," in *Uncoverings 1984*, ed. Sally Garoutte (Mill Valley, CA: American Quilt Study Group, 1985), 19–22.

23. Martha Bottoms Hammack, interview with author, Sept. 1989. Martha remembers that her mother, Nettie Goodwin Bottoms, a fine quiltmaker, had herself intended to make a *Lifeboat*.

24. Michael Luster, *Stitches in Time: A Legacy of Ozark Quilts* (Rogers, AR: Rogers Historical Museum, 1986), 5–6.

25. Ruth Haislip Roberson, ed. *North Carolina Quilts* (Chapel Hill: University of North Carolina Press, 1988), 108.

Part II: Pieced and Appliquéd Quilts

1. Schnuppe von Gwinner, *The History of the Patchwork Quilt* (Westchester, PA: Schiffer, 1988), 19.

2. *Ibid.*, 82, 85.

3. *Ibid.*, 155.

4. *An American Sampler: Folk Art from the Shelburne Museum* (Washington, DC: National Gallery of Art, 1987), 164–65.

5. Collection of Murphy family records, Atlanta, GA. Courtesy Sara Murphy.

6. *Hope Winslow's Quilt Book* (Chicago: Needleart, 1933), no. 1310, 4.

7. Mary Elizabeth Johnson, *A Garden of Quilts* (Birmingham, AL: Oxmoor House, 1984), 5. Johnson found four quilts of that vintage

"within a 100 mile radius of Greenville, Alabama." At least two were made in blue, white, and tan or unstable red now faded to "a nice camel color," the same as Jerusha's quilt. Johnson's pattern is for appliqué, "for ease in construction," because "it would be almost impossible to achieve the curves" except by hand-piecing. The pieced pattern was also found listed in Talula's copy of a 1928 Ladies Art Company catalog, pattern no. 453.

8. Letter, Mrs. J. A. Thompson, Bolivar, NY, to Talula Bottoms, 13 Oct. 1937.

9. The early Ladies Art Company pattern no. 37 was republished in several periodicals in the 1930s. Barbara Brackman's *Encyclopedia of Pieced Quilt Patterns* lists it as no. 2601.

10. Almira Bottoms Butler, *Bottoms Families in America and Descendants* (self-published, 1963), 253–259.

11. Carlie Sexton, "Yesterday's Quilts in Homes of Today," *Successful Farming*, 1930, 7.

12. *Synchronicity* is the term Carl Gustav Jung coined to explain meaningful coincidence, "when events in the outer world coincided meaningfully with inner psychic states—sometimes with a numinous impact on the individual." Edward F. Edinger, M.D., "An Outline of Analytical Psychology," reprinted from *Quadrant* (New York: C. G. Jung Foundation for Analytical Psychology, 1983), np.

Part III: Appliqued Quilts

1. *See* Michael Luster, *Stitches in Time*, 35–36; (Rogers, AR, Rogers Historical Museum, 1986) 35–36; *see also* Thomas K. Woodward and Blanche Greenstein, *Twentieth-Century Quilts: 1900–1950* (New York: E. P. Dutton, 1988), 66

2. Woodward and Greenstein, *Twentieth-Century Quilts*, 31. *See also* Brackman, *Clues in the Calico*, 155.

3. Merikay Waldvogel, *Soft Covers for Hard Times: Quiltmaking and the Great Depression* (Nashville: Rutledge Hill, 1990), ix.

4. Letter, Talula Bottoms to Mollie Ruth Bottoms, 11 Dec. 1940. *See also* Burdick, *Legacy*, 90–92.

5. Meyer, "Early Influences," 46. One striking machine-appliquéd *Orange Blossom* quilt made in Alabama by Nancy Jane Nichols Butler (c. 1890) disappointed the granddaughter who inherited it until she realized its uniqueness as a period piece (Ruth B. Potts, interview with author, 1 July 1990).

BIBLIOGRAPHY

*Beyer, Jinny. *The Quilter's Album of Blocks and Borders*. McLean, VA: EPM Publications, 1980.

Binney, Edward III, and Gail Binney Winslow. *Homage to Amanda: Two Hundred Years of American Quilts*. San Francisco: R. K. Press, 1984.

*Bishop, Robert. *The Romance of the Double Wedding Ring*. New York: E. P. Dutton, The Museum of American Folk Art, 1989.

Bottoms, Mollie Ruth. Letters. Gilbert and Bottoms Family Papers, 1827–1946.

———. Journals and Letters, 1924–1976.

Brackman, Barbara. *Clues in the Calico*. McLean, VA: EPM Publications, 1989.

———. *An Encyclopedia of Pieced Quilt Patterns*. Lawrence, KS: Prairie Flower Publishing, 1984.

Burdick, Nancilu B. Collection of Gilbert and Bottoms Family Records and Artifacts, 1827–1945.

———. *Legacy: The Story of Talula Gilbert Bottoms and Her Quilts*. Nashville: Rutledge Hill, 1988.

———. "Talula Gilbert Bottoms and Her Quilts," in *Uncoverings 1984*. Ed. Sally Garoutte. Mill Valley, CA: American Quilt Study Group, 1985.

Butler, Almira Bottoms. *Bottoms Families in America and Descendants*. Self-published, 1963.

Butler, Mary Alice. Collection of Bottoms Family Photographs and Letters.

*Carroll, Amy, ed. *The Pattern Library: Patchwork and Appliqué*. New York: Ballantine, 1981.

Cohen, Harold, Ph.D. Lecture introducing TAAP, an architecture course for volunteers. State University of New York, Buffalo, Sept. 1983.

Cooper, Patricia, and Norma Bradley Buferd. *The Quilters: Women and Domestic Art—An Oral History*. New York: Doubleday, 1977.

Dunton, William Rush, M.D. *Old Quilts*. Cantonsville, MD: Self-published, 1946.

Edinger, Edward F., M.D. "An Outline of Analytical Psychology," in *Quadrant*. New York: C. G. Jung Foundation for Analytical Psychology, 1983.

Ferraro, Pat, Elaine Hedges, and Julie Silber. *Hearts and Hands: The Influence of Women and Quilts on American Society*. San Francisco: Quilt Digest Press, 1987.

Finley, Ruth E. *Old Patchwork Quilts and the Women Who Made Them*. 1929. Reprint. Newton Center, MA: Charles T. Bradford, 1983.

Gordon, Caroline, and Allen Tate. *The House of Fiction*. New York: Charles Scribner's Sons, 1960.

Haley, Alex. *Roots*. New York: Doubleday, 1976.

Hall, Carrie A., and Rose G. Kretsinger. *The Romance of the Patchwork Quilt in America*. Caldwell, ID: Caxton Printers, 1935.

Heinburg, Richard. "Looking Back from the End of Time," *Integrity*, 100 Mile House, BC.: Integrity International, Jan.–Feb. 1987.

Hill, Sallie F. "Eight Star Designs for Patchwork Quilts," *Progressive Farmer and Southern Ruralist*, Birmingham, nd.

Hillman, James. *Healing Fiction*. Barrytown, NY: Station Hill, 1983.

*Hinson, Delores. *Quilting Manual*. New York: Dover, 1980.

Hope Winslow's Quilt Book. Chicago: Needleart, 1933.

Johnson, Mary Elizabeth. *A Garden of Quilts*. Birmingham: Oxmoor House, 1984.

Kirkpatrick, Erma. "Progressive Farmer Quilt References," in *Uncoverings 1985*. Ed. Sally Garoutte. Mill Valley, CA: American Quilt Study Group, 1986.

Langellier, Kristen. "Contemporary Quiltmaking Culture in Maine: Tradition and Transition." Paper presented at American Quilt Study Group Symposium, San Rafael, CA, 1990.

Luster, Michael. *Stitches in Time: A Legacy of Ozark Quilts*. Rogers, AR: Rogers Historical Museum, 1986.

*McClun, Diana, and Laura Nownes. *Quilts! Quilts! Quilts!: The Complete Guide to Quiltmaking*. San Francisco: The Quilt Digest Press, 1988.

Meyer, Suellen, "Early Influences of the Sewing Machine and Visible Machine Stitching on Nineteenth-Century Quilts," in *Uncoverings 1989*. Ed. Laurel Horton. San Francisco: American Quilt Study Group, 1990.

Miller, Dianne. "Machine Piecing," *Quilter's Newsletter*, July–Aug. 1989.

Murphy, Sara. Collection of Murphy Family Records.

Naisbitt, John. *Megatrends*. New York: Warner, 1984.

Olsen, Tillie. *Silences*. New York: Dell, 1965.

Olson, Charles. *A Special View of History*. Ed. Ann Charters. Berkeley: OYEZ, 1970.

Orlofsky, Patsy, and Myron Orlofsky. *Quilts in America*. New York: McGraw-Hill, 1974.

Pearson, Bettie Butler. Collection of Butler and Bottoms Family Papers and Artifacts, 1900–1948.

Potts, Ruth B. Collection of Talula Gilbert Bottoms's Quilt Patterns, Leaflets, Newspaper Clippings, and photographs.

Pozner, Vladimir. *Parting with Illusions*. New York: The Atlantic Monthly Press, 1990.

*Ramsey, Bets. *Old & New Quilt Patterns in the Southern Tradition*. Nashville: Rutledge Hill Press, 1987.

Regan, Jennifer. *American Quilts: A Sampler of Quilts and Their Stories*. New York: W. H. Smith, 1989.

Richards, Mary Caroline. *Centering in Poetry, Pottery, and the Person*. Middletown, CT: Wesleyan University Press, 1964.

Roberson, Ruth Haislip, ed. *North Carolina Quilts*. Chapel Hill: University of North Carolina Press, 1988.

Scheuer, Jeffrey. "An Interview with Allan Gurganus," *Poets and Writers*, Nov.–Dec. 1990.

Sexton, Carlie. "Yesterday's Quilts in Homes of Today," *Successful Farming*, 1930.

Von Gwinner, Schnuppe. *The History of the Patchwork Quilt*. Westchester, PA: Schiffer, 1987.

Waldvogel, Merikay. *Soft Covers for Hard Times: Quilt-Making and the Great Depression*. Nashville: Rutledge Hill Press, 1990.

Webster, Marie D. *Quilts: Their Story and How to Make Them*. New York: Doubleday, Page, & Company, 1915. Reprint. Notes and bibliography by Rosalind W. Perry. Santa Barbara, CA: Practical Patchwork, 1990.

Wilson, Florence Y. "Why Thanksgiving Day Is Perennial," *Quilter's Newsletter*, Nov. 1972.

*Wiss, Audrey, and Douglas Wiss. *Folk Quilts and How to Recreate Them*. Pittstown, NJ: Main Street Press, 1983.

Woodward, Thomas K., and Blanche Greenstein. *Twentieth-Century Quilts: 1900–1950*. New York: E. P. Dutton, 1988.

Woolf, Virginia. *A Room of One's Own*. New York: Harcourt, Brace, and World, 1929.

———

The ★ indicates useful resources for directions in making quilts.

INDEX